WISDOM

FROM THE
ANCIENTS

WISDOM

FROM THE
ANCIENTS

ENDURING BUSINESS LESSONS FROM
ALEXANDER THE GREAT, JULIUS CAESAR, AND THE
ILLUSTRIOUS LEADERS OF ANCIENT GREECE AND ROME

THOMAS J. FIGUEIRA · T. COREY BRENNAN
RACHEL HALL STERNBERG · EDITED BY JULIA HESKEL

PERSEUS
PUBLISHING

Many of the designations used by manufacturers and sellers to distinguish their products are claimed as trademarks. Where those designations appear in this book and Perseus Publishing was aware of a trademark claim, the designations have been printed in initial capital letters.

A CIP catalog record for this book is available from the Library of Congress.
ISBN 0-7382-0373-4

Perseus Publishing is a member of the Perseus Books Group.

Find us on the World Wide Web at http://www.perseuspublishing.com

Perseus Publishing books are available at special discounts for bulk purchases in the U.S. by corporations, institutions, and other organizations. For more information, please contact the Special Markets Department at the Perseus Books Group, 11 Cambridge Center, Cambridge, MA 02142, or call (617) 252–5298.

Text design by Jeffrey P. Williams
Set in 11-point Bembo by Perseus Publishing Services

First printing, October 2001
1 2 3 4 5 6 7 8 9 10—04 03 02 01

CONTENTS

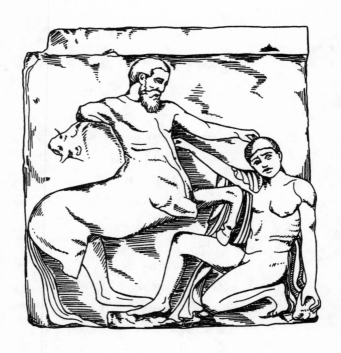

INTRODUCTION

This work arises out of the essence of our cultural heritage. The foundations of modern European and North American civilization lie in the societies of the ancient Greeks and Romans. They were our predecessors who first lived in states made up of citizens with complex social behaviors and fought struggles (sometimes all too savage) over the nature of a good and just way of living. Preeminently, they articulated their political values and beliefs in writing and codified them in law. The political ideals that in time animated the American founding fathers had their roots in the political orders of classical antiquity. Unsurprisingly, concepts that are now essential to political culture, such as politics, legislation, and democratic and republican forms of government, were formulated in the ancient world. Since the very notion of secular leadership is fundamentally an inheritance from ancient classical civilization, any consideration of the nature of leadership can profit from a long and studied glance at the experiences of the Greeks and Romans.

Naturally, management is a particular mode of leadership that we apply to the enterprises that supply both the material goods and the manifold services that characterize modern industrial and consumerist economies. Our material culture exploits mechanization of production, scientific technology, mechanical means of transportation, and instantaneous mass communication. That means that we can produce exponentially greater amounts of products and services than the Greeks and Romans and also that we are able to manipulate our environment much more dramatically than earlier people (even than those living a few centuries ago).

Because of the primitive methods and technology available for agriculture in the ancient world, most people living in premodern societies were necessarily involved in agriculture in a very hands-on fashion. Even our surviving family farms are much more productive and sophisticated establishments than the smallholdings of the ancient farmers that formed that backbone of the citizenry of classical city-states. To approximate the ancients' life experience, we would do better to think about frontier farmers in colonial America. Moreover, most establishments producing goods in the ancient Mediterranean were quite modest in scale. Ancient nonagricultural workplaces were a bit more like the workshops of contemporary artisans (such as those operating at an area crafts fair) than like the factories that typified much twentieth-century production. These conditions apply despite many parallels, such as money, banks, investments, and elaborate maritime commerce.

It is telling that we derive our term *economics* (the discipline dealing with the creation, distribution, and consumption of goods) from the Greek work *oikonomika,* which means the study of household management, and our word *economy* from *oikonomia,* meaning the management of a household, for *oikos* is a house or household and *nomoi* are laws or rules. Accordingly, when Xenophon, an Athenian soldier, writer, and a friend of Socrates, wanted to provide a guide for managing one's estate, he called it the *Oikonomikos,* or *The Household Manager.* When the great philosopher Aristotle and his students in the Lyceum, the philosophical school he founded, wanted to collect and systematize material on public management, they called their treatise the

Oikonomika. In fact, small-scale, domestic administration so prevailed in the Greek way of looking at things that they tended to extrapolate up the hierarchy of magnitude from the ordinary household. They spoke not only of domestic or city *oikonomia* or management, but also of the *oikonomia* of the controllers of larger units. These were *satraps,* the governors that the king of Persia placed over whole conquered peoples in the Near East, and the "Great King" himself, the Persian *shah* who was the master of the world's largest empire.

Hence, most of what ancient writers said about management has been derived from the political and military sphere of action rather than from the various forms of "household management" that have just been mentioned. This work will not neglect ancient advice on business in a stricter sense, however. For example, we will revisit our new friend Xenophon on a number of occasions for his wisdom on handling business affairs. We shall also better understand how to lead from the thoughts and careers of controversial personalities such as Alexander the Great and Julius Caesar, whom no one could keep down on the farm, or like Socrates, whose neglect of his stoneworking shop aroused the ire of his nagging wife. Although we have mixed in some philosophical analysis on management, much of the advice comes either in the form of admonition from the great minds of antiquity or in the form of anecdotes. Ancient authors knew how to let events, with a little creative massaging, educate on their own. Indeed, many of these stories have a liveliness and wit that transcend any single reading of their message.

A long-standing debate among ancient historians—its beginnings go well back into the nineteenth century—has been fought between scholars called *modernists,* who emphasize the aspects of ancient economies that seem most comparable to more recent conditions, and the *primitivists,* who find stronger parallels for Greek and Roman society in village-based subsistence economies. Without burdening our discussion with the technical details of these controversies, we have tried to be mindful at all times not to overpersuade the reader of the nature of the similarities between ancient and modern business conditions. We also believe that you can be trusted not to envisage your salaried workforce as slaves purchased in southern Russia or Sicily, without needing periodic sermons from us about the more exploitative and less attractive features of classical civilization. Much of the good sense of the Greeks and Romans that we include has to do with the one constant of business, management, and leadership: the human factor. The most valuable asset of any enterprise continues to be its human resources.

We start our work with some observations on the nature of leadership in the broadest sense, including style, motivation, and charisma. Then we proceed to the topic of building a team to undertake the tasks we have set ourselves. A review of building constituencies gives way to the techniques for sustaining the image of the leader and ancient advice on networking. Next we assess the converse of the same issue by exploring classical wisdom on how a leader loses his team. Then a consideration of consultation and decisionmaking is presented, including the question about when one needs to accept further input and when to close the debate. Strategy and defining objectives is next approached, where we shall include the Greek and Roman views on attitudes to take toward competition.

Ancient literature is then examined on the all-important matter of coping with competition, including negotiation and the crucial "art of the deal." Since competition puts stress on leaders and their enterprises, we segue into an examination of collegiality and teamwork that opens with some thoughts on ancient business ethics. Two chapters on entrepreneurship come in sequence: The Greeks and Romans give us some lessons first about risk taking and risk management; the focus then falls on the identification of opportunities and the skills needed to take them. Some ancient advice on communication then absorbs our interest. In further succession a series of chapters explores ancient thoughts on the work-force. First we look at how to handle manager/employee relations to achieve the most productivity. That leads to the subject of how to offer incentives and to provide compensation for employees. Next we learn the Greek and Roman attitudes toward hiring and firing. Finally, the delicate matter of delegating authority to subordinates is broached. This book closes with some final ancient instructions on how to handle success and cope with mistakes and failure.

This book has been written with the nonspecialist in mind, so we have tried to put everyone and everything into a context as we have progressed, without assuming a professorial mantle and intoning in the manner of the lecture hall. A list of significant names offers a handy reference for background on important authors and historical personages. A comprehensive time line has been provided to offer assistance on the placement of our major characters and authors in their political and cultural setting, with reference to crucial historical events.

The resources for further exploration of the material in this book are considerable. For a start, additional information on most of the persons, places, and institutions mentioned below can be conveniently sought in the third edition of the *Oxford Classical Dictionary* (1996). Two reference works published in Cambridge in England are also helpful resources: for authors, *The Cambridge History of Classical Literature* (1985), and for additional historical discussion, the second edition of *The Cambridge Ancient History* (1970–2002). Complete texts (with English translation) of most of the ancient authors found in this volume can be found in the Loeb Classical Library Series, published by Harvard University Press. More specifically, the 1897 *Dictionary of Quotations (Classical)* of T. B. Harbottle is still the best collection of its type available, and indeed has suggested to us some passages for comment.

We have collaborated on this volume, although Brennan undertook the lead for "leadership," "consulting and decisionmaking," "strategy," "risk taking," and "delegation." Sternberg was the lead author for "communication," "management/employee relations," "motivation," "hiring and firing," and "handling success and coping with mistakes." Figueira dealt with "building and losing constituencies," "competition," "collegiality and teamwork," and "recognizing opportunity."

—THOMAS FIGUEIRA

1

Leadership

I magine a personal library shelf packed with popular how-to books on leadership. If you pick up a random volume, you may find talk of the compassionate leader, or leadership by character, or principle-based leadership, or the empowerment of one's followers, or ways to gain leadership credibility. You are bound to encounter plenty of anecdotes or case studies, and the text will certainly be peppered with authoritative pronouncements and easy-to-remember lists. Yet observe that this personal library is illuminated by oil lamps and that the how-to books are written on papyrus scrolls, for we have just described the leadership literature of ancient Rome's imperial era. If it sounds familiar, it should, because the genre is still flourishing today. And if there is one point on which millennial moderns and ancients agree, it is that much of the obscure art and science of leadership can indeed be taught.

Pericles of Athens, Alexander the Great, Julius Caesar, and Caesar's adoptive son, the emperor Augustus, are just four of the most famous names that writers of Greece and Rome offered—and continue to offer—to the eager student of effective leadership. In the ancient leadership literature, dozens of other names were dragged in to serve as paradigms, whether positive or (like Pyrrhus and his "victories") negative. The subjects came from all stations of life: At the lower (indeed, lowest) end of the social spectrum, there is Spartacus, an ex-gladiator who in the mid-70s B.C., starting with just seventy-odd followers, led the deadliest slave revolt in Roman history—indeed, in all antiquity.

Homer's Multitalented Leaders

In our impressionistic sketch of the ancients on leadership, let us begin where the ancients would, with Homer's *Iliad,* an epic poem of (probably) the eighth century B.C. In a nutshell, the background to the *Iliad* goes something like this. A young man named Paris abducted the beautiful Helen from Sparta in mainland Greece and removed her to his native Troy (in the northwest of modern Turkey). Helen's brother-in-law Agamemnon mobilized and then headed the massive Greek expedition to get her back. A ten-year war followed, culminating with a ruse (the famous hollow Trojan horse) that allowed the Greeks to sack Troy. Now, Agamemnon must have had some significant leadership skills to pull off that enterprise, traditionally dated to the late thirteenth or early twelfth century B.C.—the first and last example of inter-Greek cooperation on that scale. His secret? One part vision, one part charisma, according to the Greek orator Isocrates (436–338 B.C.):

> Agamemnon was so supremely confident that it was not enough for him to levy as soldiers all the private citizens he wished from each [Greek] state. He even persuaded kings—men who used to do whatever they pleased in their own states, giving orders to everyone else—to make themselves subordinate to him, to follow him against whomever he should lead them, to obey his orders, to abandon their royal lifestyle, and to live like common soldiers. Moreover, Agamemnon persuaded them to face danger and wage war, not for their own

homelands and kingdoms, but ostensibly for Helen, wife of
Menelaus—though in reality for Greece.

—ISOCRATES, *PANATHENAICUS* (12) 79–80

Any effective large organization, Agamemnon realized, has
to be an array of smaller commands. However, despite the
presence of all those executive vice-presidents, Agamemnon's
camp was far from an "empowered workplace" in which
everyone had a say. As we see in the *Iliad*, the Greek hero
Odysseus, to keep his boss's meeting on track, uses two dis-
tinct, status-specific approaches. The senior executives get his
message, but those lower down the corporate ladder sometimes had to get his stick:

Good sir, keep yourself still and hear the speeches of others,
who are better than you, while you are unwarlike and weak,
neither to be counted ever in battle or in council.
In no way shall we Achaeans [that is, Greeks] all be kings here.
Multiple rule is no good thing! Let there be one ruler,
one king, to whom the child of Kronos the devious [that is,
Zeus] has given scepter and legal authority in order that he
deliberate for his own people.

—HOMER, *ILIAD* 2.200–206

By the way, that line "let there be one ruler" seems to have
been a favorite of ancient despots. Oligarchs "understood
nothing else in Homer," according to Aristotle's leading pupil,
Theophrastus (*Characters* 29). The implication is that Homer's
Iliad and its story of the Trojan War offers a virtual textbook
on all sorts of other matters. That is why, we are told,
Alexander the Great slept with the *Iliad* each night:

He was by his nature a lover of literature, of learning and of
reading. Thinking—and calling—the *Iliad* "a portable treasury

of military excellence," he took up the copy corrected by Aristotle, which people call the casket copy, and always kept it with a dagger under his pillow.

—PLUTARCH, *LIFE OF ALEXANDER* 8.2

Earlier than Alexander, in the late fifth century B.C., the ambitious young Athenian named Alcibiades (451–404 B.C.)—a hard-drinking aristocratic rogue, Olympic victor, diplomat, general, and sometime exile—decided he was not going to settle for an education that consisted of anything less:

When Alcibiades was getting past boyhood, he appeared before a school-teacher and asked him for a book of Homer. When the teacher replied that he had no Homer, Alcibiades punched him and left.

—PLUTARCH, *LIFE OF ALCIBIADES* 7.1

One thing that such ancient students of the *Iliad* will have noticed is that Homeric heroes—at least the best of them—were multitalented. Homer especially represents rhetorical abilities as desirable in a leader. Take Nestor, from the southwestern Peloponnese in Greece:

sweet of speech, the clear-voiced orator of the Pylians, from whose tongue flowed a voice sweeter than honey.

—HOMER, *ILIAD* 1.247–249

Or from Aetolia in north-central Greece, Thoas,

a man handy with the javelin, and who was good also in a close fight, whereas in council few surpassed him, when young men were battling in argument.

—HOMER, *ILIAD* 15.282–284

The same attributes can be found in the heroes fighting on the Trojan side. Consider Troy's ally Sarpedon, praised for his "judgments and his might" (Homer, *Iliad* 16.542), that is, his brains and his brawn. Furthermore, a hero who is weak in an essential leadership quality sometimes pairs up with someone who can complement him, as in this Trojan tandem team: "wise Polydamas . . . who was a comrade of Hector, and on the same night they were born: however one excelled in speech, the other with the spear" (Homer, *Iliad* 18.249–252).

Laundry Lists for Good Leaders

One day when Socrates met a man who had been elected general, he asked him, "For what reason, do you think, does Homer call Agamemnon 'Shepherd of the people'? . . . Or why ever did he praise Agamemnon with the words 'He was both things, a good king and a strong spearman'?" . . . [Giving the answer himself, Socrates explained] "It's because a king is chosen, not to take good care of himself, but that those who have chosen him may prosper through his agency. And all men fight, in order that they may have the best life possible, and they choose generals to serve as leaders toward this goal."

—XENOPHON, *SOCRATIC MEMOIRS* 3.2.1–3

That, at any rate, is the tale the writer Xenophon (born in Athens circa 430 B.C.) tells in his book of recollections about Socrates. It's a remarkably snappy description of the Socratic method, that is, the persuasive technique that generates a whole series of questions, to each of which there is just one reasonable answer, all building toward a grand (sometimes paradoxical) conclusion. Here Socrates takes a minimalistic stance on leadership, namely "the power to make one's followers happy." Earlier in that work Xenophon has Socrates (who wrote nothing himself) speak more expansively on the topic. Learning that a young acquaintance had paid good money to take lessons in generalship and was taught only tactics, Socrates retorts:

> A general . . . must be crafty, energetic, careful, tough and quick witted; both gentle and brutal, simultaneously straightforward and scheming, a guard and a thief, lavish and rapacious, munificent and grasping, defensive and aggressive. And there are many other attributes, owed either to nature or to study, that the individual who would be a great general must have.
>
> —XENOPHON, *SOCRATIC MEMOIRS* 3.2.6

Checklists like that ascribed to Socrates were swelling to book-length proportions by the fourth century B.C., and help form a tradition that stretched to Machiavelli and his treatise *The Prince* in the early sixteenth century (famous for its ruthless advice), and of course well beyond. The ancient appetite for leadership gurus was in fact insatiable:

> I think one must be mindful of brevity, for the sake of busy men. For it is time-consuming to hunt down individual examples, scattered over the vast body of history books. As for those who have extracted notable deeds into digests, they have overwhelmed the reader by heaping on the material.
>
> —FRONTINUS, *STRATAGEMS* 1 PREFACE

So writes Sextus Julius Frontinus (died circa A.D. 103–104), in the preface to his case study volume on what to do before, during, and after a battle. There is no shortage of such professional treatises from the ancient world. But on the topic of leadership, it is perhaps a certain Onasander, a Greek writing during the Roman empire, in his treatise *The General* (mid–first century A.D.) who is one of the more systematic in his definition:

> I say that the choice of a general is made not with an eye to noble birth . . . nor because of wealth . . . but because he is temperate, self-controlled, vigilant, frugal, weathered, has his wits about him, is free of greed, neither young nor too old, perhaps also a father of children, an adequate orator, and of good repute. . . . The general who is chosen must be honest, affable, ready for action, unflappable, not so gentle as to be despised, nor so terrifying as to be hated, so that his camp is not made lax by his favors, nor is estranged through fear.
>
> —ONASANDER, *THE GENERAL* 1.1, 2.2

Of all those qualities, alertness counts more than most, for that is what comes in handy when imponderables arise:

> The general must be sharp—as Homer says, "as a bird, or as thought," darting in his swiftness of mind at every matter. Many times unanticipated disturbances arise which force him to devise off-the-cuff what is expedient."
>
> —ONASANDER, *THE GENERAL* 1.7

Two Athenian Empire Builders

An ability to deal with the unforeseen formed a good part of the genius of the resourceful Themistocles, who engineered the great Greek naval victory over the Persians at Salamis (480 B.C.). It is for his adaptability and foresight that Thucydides, the great historian of late fifth-century Athens, singles out Themistocles as the quintessential Athenian leader of the earlier fifth century:

> Thanks to his own native intelligence, and not deliberate study at any point in his career, he was both the wisest in emergency situations where minimal deliberation is possible, and the best conjecturer of what the future will bring, even in the longest

term. . . . In brief . . . he was most excellent at improvising solutions to pressing problems.

—THUCYDIDES, *THE PELOPONNESIAN WAR* 1.138.3

Yet Themistocles never won the total loyalty of his people. He fell out of favor in his native Athens, suffering ostracism, a form of exile lasting ten years. Themistocles never returned. Rather, he ended up offering his considerable talents at the court of his former adversary, the Persian king Xerxes. In Wall Street terms, it must have been a bit like being demoted from a powerful banking position at Morgan Stanley, and then showing up as head of the same department at rival Goldman Sachs.

Compare Themistocles with Pericles, who died a generation later, in 429 B.C. Pericles led Athens for more than three decades, not just during its heady days of political power and material prosperity, but also in the first dark years of the Peloponnesian War against Sparta and her allies. In Aristotle's estimation, Pericles combined superb political vision with a larger regard for his people, and offered an example to managers and politicians alike:

We consider Pericles and the like prudent, because they are capable of examining what things are good for themselves and for mankind. We regard such individuals as experts in domestic economy and political science.

—ARISTOTLE, *NICOMACHEAN ETHICS* 1140B

Thucydides goes into some detail in trying to account for Pericles' success with the notoriously fickle Athenian democracy. For this historian, Pericles' psychological skills are grounded in a moral vision:

Pericles, who was powerful because of his reputation, judgment, and conspicuous incorruptibility, had the multitude freely in his control. He led them instead of the other way round. Because he was not one to acquire power using unseemly methods, he said nothing to flatter them; on the contrary, thanks to his standing he was able to reply to them angrily. Whenever he saw them inappropriately and arrogantly in high spirits, just by speaking he used to strike them with terror. On the other hand, if they felt irrational fear, he restored their courage. So what was ostensibly a democracy was in reality rule by the first citizen.

—THUCYDIDES, *THE PELOPONNESIAN WAR*, 2.65.8–9

Pericles clearly was gifted with an extraordinary sense of balance, and an unusually empathic style that made for inspiring and effective leadership. But then look what happened with Pericles' successors. Thucydides succinctly characterizes their management of the state as unprincipled, self-interested demagoguery:

Being more evenly matched to one another, and each grasping to be Number One, so as to please the masses they ended up entrusting even state affairs to them. From this arose many errors, since it was a great city and one that held an empire.

—THUCYDIDES 2.65.10–11

Cicero's Four Secrets of the Highly Effective Leader

Thucydides obviously put a lot of thought into what qualities make for effective leadership, providing lucid positive and negative examples. As we have seen, many later pundits would follow his cue. In the mid–first century B.C., the Roman Republican orator and statesman Marcus Tullius Cicero could even speak of a "popular" conception of the attributes of a good leader:

> Hard work in one's affairs, resolution in dangerous situations, energy in acting, speed in executing, good sense in foreseeing.
>
> —CICERO, *ON THE COMMAND OF POMPEY THE GREAT* 29

Cicero in fact expands the list for the ideal (military) leader, to add a human—indeed, moral—dimension, which is not entirely independent from what we've already seen:

> How great should be the incorruptibility of generals, how great their self-restraint in all things! How great their good faith, their affability, their natural faculties, their human touch!
>
> —CICERO, *ON THE COMMAND OF POMPEY THE GREAT* 36

But when push comes to shove, in Cicero's own humble opinion:

> I am of the conviction that a top-rate general needs to have these four things: knowledge of military affairs, high character, authority, and good fortune.
>
> —CICERO, *ON THE COMMAND OF POMPEY THE GREAT* 28

The Leader's Personal Touch

The ideal requirements for Rome's top leaders had changed somewhat by the time of the emperor Hadrian (A.D. 117–138), who ruled at the height of Roman imperial power. This emperor counted as his main concern the stability of Rome's territorial empire, not its expansion under his personal military command. To achieve such stability, a complex skill mix was needed. Hadrian managed to impress his subordinates not by martial prowess but by sheer smarts, affability, a talent for getting names straight, and an amazing facility for multitasking:

In conversation even with folks of the lowest rank, Hadrian maintained the utmost of civility. He hated people of the type who begrudged him this natural pleasure, under the guise of protecting the emperor's dignity. . . . His memory was superb, and there was no end to his eloquence: for he personally composed his own speeches and all responses to petitions. . . . Without aid from a prompter, he rattled off many individuals' names which he had heard just once and as part of a group. The upshot was that rather frequently he corrected the [professional] nomenclators when they made a mistake. He called by name all the old veterans whom he had discharged at one time or other. . . . Simultaneously, he wrote, dictated, listened to others, and chit-chatted with friends.

—*HISTORIA AUGUSTA, LIFE OF HADRIAN* 20.1, 6–7, 9–11

Somewhat earlier, from the restless island province known as Britain, comes an ancient exemplar of good MBWA (management by walking around). The Roman historian Tacitus had an uncle, Agricola, who found himself as governor of that rainy island in the A.D. 80s. Agricola had a hard-driving management style, but we are told that his hands-on approach and innate sense of fairness made his manner that much easier to swallow:

Starting with himself and his staff, he kept his household in check—a thing which most men find no less difficult than governing a province. He did not use freedmen and slaves to

transact official business. Nor did he select his centurions or soldiers on the basis of letters of recommendation or personal entreaties. Rather, he considered the most reliable man to be the best one in each case. . . . When summer came, he collected his army and fully joined them on their maneuvers, praising those who exercised self-restraint, and bringing stragglers back into the fold. He himself designated the site of the camp, and personally performed the reconnaissance of estuaries and forests. Meanwhile, he allowed the enemy to have no rest, devastating their lands by sudden raids. And when he had sufficiently terrified the enemy, conversely by sparing them he showed them the attractions of peace.

—TACITUS, *LIFE OF AGRICOLA* 19.2, 20.2

Agricola, we are told, even gave assistance to these former enemies in the building of temples, forums, and houses. It comes as no surprise that the importance of setting a good example shows up also in the ancient leadership treatises:

If the general is in a rush to finish a project he has in hand, he should not be slow to be especially conspicuous in doing it. For it is not so much threats from immediate superiors as the persuasions of leading men that compel soldiers to activity. For when a soldier sees that his commander is the first to put his hand to the task, he realizes the need for speed, is ashamed not to take action, and is afraid to disobey orders. Furthermore, the rank and file are no longer treated like a slave under orders, but are persuaded, by a peer's encouragement.

—ONASANDER, *THE GENERAL* 42.2

For putting those precepts into action, it is hard to top Alexander the Great. Stories of his great leadership abilities abound. Take, for example, the story of how in 330 B.C. he motivated his troops to persist in their pursuit of the conquered Persian king Darius. Parched with thirst, having marched 400 miles over hostile terrain in the space of eleven days,

It happened that some Macedonians encountered Alexander as they fetched water from a river in skins upon their mules. They saw him in a bad way from thirst (for it was about noon), and they quickly filled up a helmet and offered it to him. Alexander asked them for whom they were fetching the water. "For our own children," they said. "But even if we should cause their death, we shall have other ones—provided that you are alive." On hearing this, Alexander took the helmet into his hands. But looking around and seeing all the horsemen about him craning their necks toward him and focussing on the helmet, he offered his thanks and gave it back without drinking, "Well, should I be the only one to drink", he said, "these men will lose heart."

—PLUTARCH, *LIFE OF ALEXANDER* 42.7–9

Management Equals Motivating?

Let's turn from that dry topic to another, the notion of business competition as warfare—nowadays practically a cliché. Indeed, wisdom from Napoleon and von Clausewitz, Eisenhower and Schwarzkopf peppers many a contemporary management book. But the ancients would have understood. In a treatise on household management by the writer Xenophon, the leisured Athenian Ischomachus describes to Socrates how leadership attributes in war and business are (or should be) the same. Indeed, in the speaker's opinion, all enterprises—agriculture, politics, estate management, warfare—share common ground. But it is the military sphere that dramatically reveals the difference between the feeble leader and the strong:

Some leaders make their men unwilling to work and to run risks, not thinking it fit to obey nor willing to do so except under compulsion, and even congratulating themselves on their opposition to their commander. And these same leaders make their men unable to understand the consequences, should anything disgraceful occur. But inspired, excellent and skilled leaders are a different matter. On taking over the same troops, or perhaps others, they have them ashamed to do anything that is base, convinced that it is better to obey, and happy to follow orders; as individuals or as an army, when it's necessary to work, the soldiers do so enthusiastically.

Ischomachus then singles out the ability to motivate, rather than simple soldierly attributes such as physical strength, as the crucial component of real leadership. Real leaders are those

who can make their soldiers feel that they must follow them through fire and in any risky enterprise. . . . So too in private industries, the person in authority—whether he be a bailiff or manager—who can make the workers enthusiastic, vigorous and persevering, that's the type of person who does good for the business and builds a large surplus.

—XENOPHON, *THE HOUSEHOLD MANAGER* 21.4–5, 7, 9

Socrates' Management Calculation

Socrates himself is said to have seen it (as so often) a different way: when it comes to leadership, managers have something to teach the military. Here he is trying to persuade a veteran officer who found himself defeated at the Athenians' annual election of generals that the businessman he lost to may in fact be more qualified for the post:

"Is it not the task of both the good business man and the good general to make their subordinates compliant and obedient?" said Socrates. "And to entrust individual matters to the individuals suitable to do them? I also think that it is incumbent on both to punish the bad and honor the good. And is it not commendable for both to make their subordinates well-disposed? Don't you think it's to the advantage of both to attract allies and helpers? Isn't it appropriate for both to guard what they possess? And just as appropriate that both be attentive and industrious in their own affairs?"

"But you leave out," replied the veteran officer, "what help business knowledge will be should it come to a fight."

"It's there where it will be most helpful. For the good business man, realizing that nothing is as advantageous and profitable as defeating one's enemies in battle, and nothing is so disadvantageous and financially ruinous as defeat, eagerly will search out and prepare what is conducive to victory, and will attentively consider and guard against what leads to defeat. Should he see that he has the resources to win, he will actively fight. But above all, if he finds himself unprepared, he will be careful not to join battle."

Socrates continued, "Don't look down on business men. For the management of private concerns differs only in respect to volume from that of public affairs. In other respects they are quite similar, especially in this regard: neither functions without the help of individuals, nor are private and public affairs transacted by different types of individuals."

—XENOPHON, *SOCRATIC MEMOIRS* 3.4.8–9, 11–12 (ABRIDGED)

In this conversation Socrates lists the ability to motivate associates and subordinates as just one of a host of business leadership qualities. What's particularly interesting is that in that last bit he comes pretty close to a common modern definition of management itself—getting things done through others—as well as offering a good description of strategic management techniques.

Adrenalin from the Arena

"The general who became a slave, the slave who became a gladiator, who defied an empire." Not too shabby a curriculum vitae. In the film *Gladiator* the core reason Maximus made things happen for himself and his various organizations (legions in Germania, gladiatorial bands in Rome) was that he was not simply a fighter, but also a strategic thinker and an effective communicator—in short, a leader.

The same goes for a historical gladiator who defied an empire, Spartacus. Starting life not as a general but as a semi-Hellenized native of Thrace (roughly, modern-day Bulgaria), he was enslaved and brought to Rome, finally ending up in a brutal gladiatorial school in southern Italy. He and about seventy-five of his companions successfully made a break from their confinement. Soon their mini-revolt mushroomed into a massive slave uprising, one that was to occupy some of Rome's best generals for two full years (73–71 B.C.). Even a full decade after the defeat and death of Spartacus, we hear of bitter-enders from his rebellion still causing trouble in Italy.

How did he do it? According to the Greek biographer Plutarch, Spartacus was conspicuous for his courage and physical strength. Yet that was true of many gladiators. Once in the amphitheater, it was felt that the least promising sort of gladiator might far exceed his perceived capabilities.

> Even among the gladiators of Caesar there are certain ones who are vexed that they are not led out and matched up. They pray to the god, they approach their handlers, begging to fight.
>
> —EPICTETUS, *DISCOURSES* 1.29.37

In a speech of A.D. 100, Pliny the Younger—senator, advocate in court, confidant of the Roman emperor Trajan—tells how he once witnessed such an exhibition, where the gladiators themselves positively wanted to fight,

> a spectacle not lifeless and weak, nor one that would soften and break the spirits of men, but one which inspired them to noble wounds and contempt for death, since in the persons of slaves

and even criminals the love of glory and the desire for victory
was discerned.

—PLINY THE YOUNGER, *PANEGYRIC ORATION* 33.1

Understandably, a few gladiators had no intention of dying
in this way, just to gratify the bloodlust of the Roman crowd.
Instead they chose alternate paths to glory, including some
pretty extreme methods of suicide.

But back to Plutarch, on Spartacus as a leader. He adds that
this gladiator also had intelligence, a refreshing lack of boor-
ishness—but not least a somewhat cultivated charisma.

The story goes that when he first was brought to
Rome to be sold, a snake was seen coiled about
his face as he slept. And his wife, who
belonged to the same nation as Spartacus,
was a prophet, and also a devotee of
the orgiastic rites of the god Dionysus,
interpreted the sign to mean that there
was a great and frightening power about
him that would lead to good issue. At the
time of the breakout from the gladiatorial
school, she was living with him and escaped with him.

—PLUTARCH, *LIFE OF CRASSUS* 8.3–4

And served a crucial role as a full-time publicity agent, we may
suspect.

Where Authority Fades into Hype

Most men are distressed when placed under the command of
ignoble individuals. For no one voluntarily puts up with sub-
mitting to a master or a leader who is a man inferior to himself.

—ONASANDER, *THE GENERAL* 1.17

So far we have looked mostly at natural or "real" leaders and their attributes. Yet when it comes to leadership, perceptions can very much make the reality, as Cicero fully realized:

> Who is not aware that in the conduct of wars it matters a lot what the enemy and what the allies think of our generals? For we know that in such serious affairs men are stirred to fear, or despise, or hate, or love a man by common opinion and rumor no less than by some consistent consideration.
>
> —CICERO, *ON THE COMMAND OF POMPEY THE GREAT* 43

In particular, personal charisma might make all the difference, as Socrates' friend Ischomachus is made to remark of an estate manager:

> Socrates, as for the master who appears at work—the person who has the capability of severely punishing the bad workers and greatly rewarding the enthusiastic ones—but whose appearance makes no difference in the workers' production, I would not want to be in his shoes. However, should they put themselves into motion on spotting him, and each of the workers grow passionate and competitive with one another and ambitious to outdo the teammates, I would say that this man has something of royal character in him. . . . I really do not think that this gift—to manage subordinates who are willing—is wholly human, but rather divine. Clearly it has been given to those genuinely devoted to sensibility.
>
> —XENOPHON, *THE HOUSEHOLD MANAGER* 21.10, 12

The Leader as Performer

For an audacious shortcut to winning obedience, consider this tale told by the historian Herodotus. It concerns how the tyrant Peisistratus, once tossed out of Athens, reestablished himself in the city shortly after 560 B.C. After contracting to marry the daughter of one Megacles (of the powerful family known as the Alcmeonids), the two men found a local woman named Phya—in a loose translation, "good-looking." They dressed up this woman in full armor, to look like Athena, the patron deity of Athens. They then made her taxi Peisistratus into the city in a chariot, while heralds proclaimed to the Athenians "to receive Peisistratus warmly, whom Athena herself, honoring him above all men, is restoring to the Acropolis." Herodotus finds the success of this ruse inexplicable, given the reputed intelligence of the Athenians. He does note, however, that Phya was extraordinarily tall by the standards of those times: the historian gives her height as five foot ten.

A much shorter individual, Alexander the Great (five foot one), early in his campaigning in Asia Minor, turned a particularly knotty problem into a public relations coup. Entering the city of Gordium, the seat of old king Midas (traditionally, 738–696 B.C.), he saw the king's chariot, with the yoke fastened by a gnarly mass of bark cords. Local legend had it that whoever could untie that knot was fated to rule Asia. Most authors tell the story that Alexander, when he found himself unable to untie the knot, simply cut it apart with his sword. So in (literally) one stroke he secured his reputation for decisiveness, boldness, and the ability to think outside of the box.

The Romans, too, had a talent for PR not unworthy of Madison Avenue. That great military man of the later Roman Republic, Gaius Marius, was to reach the highest office in the land (the consulship) an unprecedented seven times in the years 107–86 B.C. Yet he was not beneath trotting out as a management aid a high-profile prophetess (a role that fell somewhere between a modern business guru and infomercial psychic) dressed in purple, who carried a little spear trimmed with ribbons and garlands.

There was a Syrian woman, by the name of Martha, said to have the gift of prophesy. Marius was in the habit of solemnly carrying her about as she reclined in a litter, and he performed sacrifice as she ordered. This woman the Senate previously had driven away, when she wished to approach it and foretell the future. Next Martha made her way to the senators' wives, and demonstrated her skill—especially to Marius's wife. Sitting beside her at the gladiatorial contests, Martha correctly predicted who would be victor; she dispatched Martha to Marius's camp, where she received marks of respect. . . . However, many found it ambiguous whether Marius genuinely fell under her persuasion, or was feigning and playing along in exhibiting the woman publicly.

—PLUTARCH, *LIFE OF MARIUS* 17.2–5

Or consider Sertorius, a rebel Roman governor of Spain who managed to hold his position for a decade, including eight years of fighting against two formidable generals (one of them Pompey). To cement his hold over the native Iberian auxiliaries, he tamed a white fawn to serve as his personal mascot. In time it answered to Sertorius's call and accompanied him on his walks. Eventually, he persuaded his superstitious troops that the fawn was a gift of the goddess Diana:

And [Sertorius] alleged that the animal revealed many hidden things to him. . . . Whenever he had secret intelligence that the enemy had attacked some part of the land under his control or had caused a city to revolt, he pretended that the doe had conversed with him in his sleep, and ordered him to have his forces ready. Or when he had word that his generals had scored a victory, he used to hide the messenger, and bring forth the doe wearing a garland to signify the good news, urging his men to be of good heart and sacrifice to the gods, since they were going to learn of something good.

—PLUTARCH, *LIFE OF SERTORIUS* 11.6–8

For the deliberate manufacture of a personality cult, the Roman Empire (especially in its later phases) offers a mine of material. When a vote by Rome's military leaders in A.D. 284 elevated Diocletian, a commander of the palace bodyguards, to the status of emperor, he went a bit overboard in personal image-building to match his job title. He was the first emperor to wear a gold-embroidered cloak and gem-studded shoes of silk and purple. More consequentially, he encouraged men to call him "lord" and "god," and to offer him corresponding honors, a type of autocratic behavior pioneered by the Roman emperors Caligula (A.D. 37–41) and Domitian (81–96). But we are told that Diocletian's good qualities balanced his bad.

Contrast, however, Commodus (reigned A.D. 180–192). That Roman emperor, through ostentatious shows of valor in (merely) the gladiatorial arena, ended up looking ridiculous—or worse:

> It is documented that under his father [Marcus Aurelius, emperor A.D. 161-180] he fought 365 times; furthermore, that for the net-fighters he defeated or killed, he later won so many gladiatorial prizes so as to reach the 1,000-mark. Plus there were many thousands of various wild animals that he killed with his own hand, even to the point of killing elephants. And these feats he performed with the Roman people often as his audience. However, though strong for these activities, in other respects Commodus was weak and feeble. He even had a problem in the area of his groin, conspicuous enough that the Roman people could see the swelling through his silk clothing. This inspired the writing of many verses.
>
> —HISTORIA AUGUSTA, LIFE OF COMMODUS 12.10–13.1

Needless to say, this is carrying the notion of leader as "performer" beyond the limit of propriety and public opinion. Indeed, PR works only to a point. The later emperor Elagabulus (A.D. 218–222)—one of Rome's worst, thanks to his obsessive devotion to a Syrian god of the same name—offended senatorial opinion in any number of ways, not least by this ill-conceived ploy to gain respectability:

When he entered either the camp or the Senate House, he also brought in his grandmother Varia, so as to improve his standing through her authority, because he was hapless on his own. Before his reign, a woman had never entered the Senate in such a manner that she was asked to draft a decree, and express an opinion.

—*HISTORIA AUGUSTA, LIFE OF HELIOGABULUS* 12.3

About three years into this emperor's bizarre reign, Granny—her proper name was Julia Maesa—cut her losses. She instead backed another grandson, Alexander Severus, seeing to his smooth accession to the throne after the Praetorian Guard murdered Elagabalus in March 222.

A Word About Luck

In the ancient view, the complete leader needed not just brains, personality, and stamina, but also good luck. Indeed, felicity was a charismatic quality about which successful Roman commanders never tired of boasting, even in official dedications, but it was a quality that could easily slip out of one's hands. Cicero makes out that he is treading a thin line in talking about the good fortune of Pompey:

Concerning the luckiness of the man presently under discussion, I will refrain from saying that good fortune was actually placed in his power. But I will speak so as to appear to remember what is past, and to have good hope of what is to come. For I do not wish that my speech seem to the immortal gods to be either arrogant or ungrateful.

—*CICERO, ON THE COMMAND OF POMPEY THE GREAT* 47

What happens when good luck turns bad? Well, take the monarch Mithridates VI of Pontus (reigned 120–63 B.C.), who operated out of the area which is now northern Turkey to make himself Rome's Public Enemy No. 1. When King Mithridates saw his own fortune fail in his war against Pompey, his most useful allies soon parted ways. That in turn prompted the king to take desperate countermeasures:

> Faced with frequent defections, and suspecting his own army . . . because soldiers always lack confidence in unlucky commanders, Mithridates had eunuchs take his daughters to marry [wavering allied] dynasts, requesting that they send him an army as quickly as possible.
>
> —APPIAN, *MITHRIDATIC WARS* 108.515–516

The upshot? The allies killed the eunuchs (Mithridates had an awful lot of them), and handed over the young women to Pompey and the Romans.

However, it's a bad idea for stakeholders to blame every failure on bad luck or "fortune."

> Stupid people blame disasters on Fortune alone, as opposed to negligence on the part of commanders, and also credit successes to her, but not to commanders' skill. It's not reasonable to let off the hook a leader who has incurred complete disaster, on the grounds that Fortune is responsible for all things. Nor is it right to overlook the successful general, leaving him so unheralded and unpraised that one offers gratitude for everything to Fortune.
>
> —ONASANDER, *THE GENERAL*, PREFACE 6

Take Crassus, who, with Pompey and Caesar, constituted the so-called "First Triumvirate" (an informal but highly effective junta) in the 50s B.C. Anxious to score a major military success so that he could put himself on the same level as his political friends, Crassus ended up picking on the wrong people—and quite literally lost his head in a battle of 53 B.C. The Greek writer Plutarch reports the public's Monday morning quarterbacking of Crassus's fatal crossing of the Euphrates River to attack the fearsome Parthians, then masters of north Mesopotamia:

> To the multitude he represented Fortune, but to the wise he was an example of thoughtlessness and excessive ambition, on account of which he did not acquiesce in being first and greatest among the countless number of men. Rather, because of the perception that he was inferior to just two men, he thought he lacked everything.
>
> —PLUTARCH, *LIFE OF CRASSUS* 27.6

Or to borrow a phrase from Voltaire, for Crassus the best really was the enemy of the good.

2

Building and Losing Constituencies

It is inevitable that ever larger enterprises develop, as the output for each worker increases both through the accumulation of more capital assets and the progress of technology. The successive stages of the process, reaching from the extraction of raw material and the marshaling of trained labor through the delivery of a usable product or service to the consumer, become more differentiated. Modern executives often find valuable lessons in the careers of the great captains and statesmen of the ancient world, whose sway encompassed great armies and powerful states comparable to our huge businesses. An important aspect of such leadership is the ability to build and sustain the collaboration and enthusiasm of individuals carrying out the necessary tasks. Morale within the enterprise is vital to that end.

Building Support

Given the constraints of human nature, the most ready means for building up a following in antiquity could not radically differ from the practices we know from our own experience. For instance, Julius Caesar exemplifies the leader who woos potential supporters by providing material inducements. His strongest lesson for us may be that it is virtually impossible to go overboard in this endeavor of offering emoluments to possible recruits. Such "gratuities," unfortunately, can be addictive.

Gladiators, Gladiators, Gladiators!

Suetonius was a biographer active around A.D. 100, who documented the lives of the first twelve Roman emperors. He had a taste for the risqué and lurid along with the public facts of his subjects' lives, so that his biographies have provided the material for Robert Graves's *I Claudius* (and its television dramatization) and countless cinema costume epics. The first biography in Suetonius's series was that of Julius Caesar. Here is his take on Caesar's recruitment of followers after election to his second consulship. Not only did he build a new forum, but he also announced gladiatorial games and a public feast for all the citizens of Rome (a first).

So that the anticipation of these events might be as great as possible, those preparations pertaining to the banquet, although contracted from caterers, he also brought to final readiness in his household. He ordered that established gladiators whenever they fought before disapproving spectators, be abducted forcibly and kept in reserve for his games. He trained rookie gladiators neither in a school nor by coaches, but in private homes by Roman knights and even by senators who were experts in arms, pressing them by entreaties (something shown by his correspondence) that they should undertake the instruction of individual trainees and personally give verbal direction to them while they went through their exercises.

—SUETONIUS, *LIFE OF JULIUS CAESAR* 26.2–3

Caesar's second method of winning favor was to provide increased governmental outlays for important constituencies, the soldiers, and the urban population. Whether viewed as setting rewards or incentives or here for its impact on subordinates, this facet of leadership lies at the center of executive management.

Laying It On with a Trowel

He doubled the pay of the [army] legions in perpetuity. However often there was a plentiful supply of grain, he made it available without limit and measure, and he periodically distributed individual slaves from prisoners of war to each Roman.

SUETONIUS, *LIFE OF JULIUS CAESAR* 26.3

Under a democratic or republican political order, one of the best ways to build support is to reward people out of their own resources. According to Athenian historical traditions, the first politician to bring this technique to the level of an art form was the great Pericles, the builder of the exquisite monuments such as the Parthenon that we associate with the golden age of classical Greece in the fifth century B.C. Vigorous males were employed by the government in its armed services. Yet Pericles was not prepared to give his people a share of the proceeds from their booming economy and overseas empire as largess, but insisted that payments be linked to the provision of services.

Workfare?

Yet Pericles, unwilling that the menial crowd incapable of mobilization have no share in revenues or that it take a share while unemployed and idle, introduced proposals before the people for vast initiatives for construction and expensive plans involving crafts over considerable blocks of time, in order that, no less than

those sailing, serving in garrisons, and going on campaigns, the
sedentary population would have a pretext for taking their share
and profiting from public resources.

—PLUTARCH, *LIFE OF PERICLES* 12.7

This program permitted Pericles to provide work for extrac-
tive industries, for crafts processing raw material, and for the
transportation sector. Our anecdote closes with a strikingly
modern picture of a large enterprise conquering the work
before it, as though it were a mighty expedition.

Each craft had marshaled under it a mass of common individual workers, comprising an instrument and body [just like a
general has his army], and the requirements for the projects distributed and sowed affluence for every age group [so to speak]
and every human endowment.

—PLUTARCH, *LIFE OF PERICLES* 12.7

It is also important to appreciate how the whole Athenian
economy benefited from the industries, professional skills, and
abilities to function cooperatively in the workplace that
Pericles called into being by his programs.

It was a classic observation that the Roman common people during the empire were kept quiescent through "bread
and circuses." One of the best formulations of the idea that
providing entertainment and diversions could actually be
more important than distributing food is found in the writings of the orator and senator Marcus Cornelius Fronto, who
lived in the second century A.D. Fronto was the tutor and
friend of the future emperor and lifelong philosopher Marcus
Aurelius. Fronto gives his views in a letter to Antoninus Pius,
the predecessor of Marcus Aurelius, from a collection called
Principles of History.

The Hell with Bread; Bring on the Circuses

[The emperor] Trajan seems to have borrowed from the best tradition of civil administration in carefully providing for actors and other artists of the stage, of the circus, and of the arena. He knew that the Roman people are captivated especially by two things, bread and games; that the government wins approval just as much through its amusements as its serious aspects; and that while neglect of serious business caused greater harm, more significant resentment was brought about by neglect of amusements. And Trajan knew that people desired games more feverishly than even distributions of money, for largess of grain and money pacified only a privileged subset of the city, individually and particularly, but games everybody.

—FRONTO, *PRINCIPLES OF HISTORY* 2.18

Unfortunately, maintaining one's support can be harder than garnering it in the first place. The precedent of past benefits arouses an expectation of the continuation of favors into the future. Then advantaged people can become jaded by the repetition of favors at the previous level, so it becomes hard to say no to additional demands. Gaius Plinius Secundus, usually called Pliny the Younger, was a prominent Roman politician of the later first and early second centuries A.D. He achieved success in several areas of public life, including advocacy in the courts, prominence as a senator, and service as a Roman provincial governor. His letters are especially valuable for their glimpses of the conditions of Roman politics as seen by an insider.

But What Have You Done for Me Lately?

Moreover, when I recalled what dangers I had undergone on behalf of these people even in my earlier advocacy, I decided that the credit of my earlier service must be preserved with a new favor. Indeed, there is a general consensus that you undermine earlier benefits unless you compound them with additional ones, for however often people have been in debt to you, once you refuse them some one thing, they remember that thing alone that has been denied to them.

—PLINY THE YOUNGER, *LETTERS* 3.4.7

The world-weary voice of a pragmatic realist comes across manifestly.

Few leaders have ever had as much impact on their society as Alcibiades, the late-fifth-century B.C. Athenian politician and general. Famous for his tutelage under his uncle Pericles and through his friendship with Socrates, Alcibiades was so charismatic that he literally seduced the Athenians, both male and female, into granting him the leading place in their society. Sadly, this combination of Elvis Presley, Bill Clinton, and Madonna came to a tragic end. His self-aggrandizement and transgressive behavior made his leadership risky not only for himself, but for his whole city. His misadventures played a large part in the defeat of the Athenians in the great Peloponnesian War with the Spartans. Hence, Alcibiades was a good subject for Plutarch's series of biographies of pairs of Greek and Roman great men. Here Plutarch tries to sum up his subject's remarkable ability for gaining support and power in whatever cultural setting he found himself.

Don't Try This at Home!

So he had, they say, a singular natural facility out of the many qualities in him, and it was a device for the pursuit of men, namely a method to assimilate and internalize men's behaviors and lifestyles by his own managing sharper transformations than a chameleon. Except that the chameleon (as is reported) is without the capacity to assimilate itself to one color, white. Yet for Alcibiades, making his way among good and bad alike, nothing was beyond imitation and not practicable. At Sparta he was athletic, self-denying, and saturnine; in [Asian] Ionia luxurious, pleasure seeking, and equable; in Thrace devoted to heavy drinking; in Thessaly part of the "horsy set"; and when he spent time with [the Persian governor] Tissaphernes, he exceeded Persian magnificence with his pretension and extravagance. He did not so easily convert himself from one style to another, nor did he absorb every transformation *within* his character. But, because by indulging his true nature, he was likely to discountenance his companions of the moment, always in every context he assumed the contours appropriate to those associates and thus a counterfeit form, avoiding self-betrayal.

—PLUTARCH, *LIFE OF ALCIBIADES* 23.4–5

Although he was already a leading politician, Alcibiades could not refrain from entirely unnecessary risks, remarkable behavior in someone who had often risked his life in battle. For example, the Athenians conducted annual sacred rites of initiation that promised their participants an exalted life after death, but only if the "mysteries" were not divulged to the uninitiated, under pain of execution. The sexual content of these mysteries may have been too tempting to Alcibiades, who "consummated" the rites privately in front of uninitiated persons. The Athenians condemned him to death, and he fled into exile. Then he defected to the enemies of Athens and used his confidential knowledge against his countrymen. Remarkably, after he had worn out his welcome in the enemy camp, he engineered a return from exile to become the supreme commander of the Athenian military. After a few years, his highhandedness led to a second exile. He was assassinated in 404 B.C. when he was planning yet another political comeback.

As the following example from the early Roman Empire indicates, adaptation to one's local environment could be a powerful technique for winning support, even in unlikely places. But the true coalition builder can't help trying. Julius Caesar Germanicus was the nephew of the emperor Tiberius and his heir apparent. He was sent to the eastern provinces of Rome to supervise their administration. In A.D. 19, shortly after his arrival in the eastern Mediterranean, Germanicus made a controversial visit to Roman-controlled Egypt. His comportment there was unwelcome to his uncle, the emperor, as this account from the *Annals* of the senator and historian Tacitus explains.

> Germanicus set out for Egypt to view its antiquities, but concern for the province was put forward as a pretext. He lowered the price of grain by throwing open the public grain warehouses, and he adopted many behaviors popular with the common people. He walked around without bodyguards, with his feet sandaled, and in dress just like the Greeks, acting in emulation of Publius Scipio [conqueror of Hannibal], whom tradition reports to have behaved the same way, although the war with Carthage was still raging.
>
> —TACITUS, *ANNALS* 2.59

There is more than a hint of disapproval here in Germanicus's quest for favor, although Tacitus is usually more sympathetic to him than to Tiberius (a particular object of his distaste). However, these Egyptian Greeks did not appear to be "players" worth wooing politically back in Rome. Germanicus's behavior went over especially poorly with his uncle the emperor, because the late emperor Augustus, Germanicus's own grandfather, had forbidden Roman senators and high-ranking knights (that is, the political and administrative leadership) from entering Egypt without permission. Augustus was afraid that a usurper would seize Egypt and cut off the flow of grain needed to feed Rome.

Making the Most of What You Have

Managers have to build constituencies among the collaborators and employees available to them, persons who might not
have been their first choice. They make the best of the material at hand, trying to compensate for individual shortcomings
by preaching self-discipline and by resolving the task at hand
into its subcomponents. Take Sertorius, a Roman general who
found himself on the losing side of a civil war that ground to
a bloody halt in Italy in 82 B.C. Sertorius attempted to maintain the Spanish provinces as a stronghold and refuge for people of his political persuasion. His Spanish allied troops were
enthusiastic but undisciplined. He allowed them to engage in
battle with his adversaries, and when they got into difficulty,
he intervened with his Italian troops to save the day. He then
turned their defeat into a lesson:

Cooperation Is Better Than Individual Showboating

Wishing to dispel their dejection, after a few days he called a
general assembly, before which he brought two horses. One was
totally weak and well past its prime, the other sizable and
strong, possessing a tail amazing for its thick, beautiful hairs. By
the side of the weak one stood a tall, powerful man; by the
strong horse another man who was small and contemptible in
appearance. Once a signal was given them, the strong man with
both hands violently dragged the horse-tail toward himself, as if
to tear it off; the weak man plucked out the hairs of the strong
horse one by one. The first individual gave up on his attempt,
after giving himself a lot of trouble for nothing (and plenty of
laughs to the audience). However the weak man quickly and
effortlessly stripped clean the horse's tail. Sertorius rose up and
said, "Look, allies: perseverance has more efficacy than brute
force, and many things that cannot be overcome when they
stand together yield to one who is systematic. Persistence is

invincible, through which time on its march captures and sub-
dues any opposing force, being a friendly ally to those deliber-
ately awaiting their opportunity.

—PLUTARCH, *LIFE OF SERTORIUS* 16. 3–5

The Spaniards took the hint and were thereafter alert to military opportunities that they needed to take in cooperation.

Sustaining the Executive Image

Just like modern executives, ancient leaders were aware of the
role impressions made on their followers. The reader may
decide whether they were fortunate or unfortunate not to
have the benefit of image gurus. As in our age of cosmetic sur-
gery and prostheses, ancient leaders were careful to project a
youthful and attractive physical persona. Let us take one
example each from the Greeks and the Romans.

In the previous chapter we noted the popularity at Athens
of the seductive Alcibiades in late-fifth-century Athens. His
uncle Pericles was undoubtedly the greater statesman, but,
when it came to his looks, he resorted to subterfuge. Pericles
had a very long head and so he tried to be portrayed wearing
a helmet, as Plutarch notes in his biography.

Don't Point That Head at Us!

The appearance of his body was in other regards unobjection-
able, but elongated and asymmetrical as regards the head.
Therefore, nearly all the representations of him are equipped
with helmets, since the craftsmen were unwilling (it appears) to
hold him up to reproach.

—PLUTARCH, *LIFE OF PERICLES* 3.2

Nor was this sensitivity mere vanity; the Greeks had long associated a sharp pointed head with tyranny. They tended to

envisage the political dictator as a sort of mutant arising out of the aristocracy, perhaps through an illicit coupling between an upper-class woman and a *déclassé* male that foisted the resultant tyrant-in-waiting on an unsuspecting "father." Comic poets, ancient equivalents of late-night show hosts like Leno and Letterman, were less concerned about Pericles' self-image and more committed to deflating political pretensions. Plutarch was able to quote four different comedies ridiculing the shape of Pericles' head (and others could be added). He also reports that, in general, the playwrights called Pericles "Squill-Head."

Hair loss troubled "alpha" males in antiquity just as now, although they lacked "hair clubs" and Rogaine to fight back. Baldness was the physical trait whose manifestation most worried Julius Caesar in the first century B.C., as the biographer Suetonius reports.

The Hair Club for Romans

He truly bore the deformity of baldness very badly, having experienced often his vulnerability to the jokes of his detractors. For that reason he was even accustomed to "recall" his thinning strands from the very top of his head, and out of all the honors decreed for him by the people and senate he neither accepted nor took advantage of any other more gladly than the right of wearing a laurel wreath on every occasion.

—SUETONIUS, *LIFE OF JULIUS CAESAR* 45.2

Roman leaders did have one large advantage over their Greek counterparts. The sway of Rome was so vast that most Roman citizens and almost all Roman subjects never got the chance to examine prominent men all that closely. Hence, Caesar's nephew, the emperor Augustus, could be portrayed as a handsome young figure indefinitely into old age.

Distance is a useful tactic, so the CEO often remains aloof from his workers and employs middle managers to do his job for him. The effect of distance could be made to work for a Roman emperor in areas of administration. During a crisis in the early first century A.D., for example, the emperor Tiberius appreciated that direct interventions were best made by surrogates like his adopted sons Drusus and Germanicus. In this way, the imperial majesty could remain a more mysterious force, held in reserve until the utmost extremity of danger to the regime and state. Tacitus, who rarely approves of Tiberius, thought worthy of praise his attitude to simultaneous enemy attacks and mutinous troops on two vital sectors of the northern frontiers.

Never Micromanage a Barbarian Horde

It was an unshakeable and fixed principle for Tiberius in the face of these speeches [of criticism] not to abandon the center of public affairs nor place himself and the state into a risky situation. Indeed, there were many and various matters giving him anxiety [like the crises in Germany and Pannonia, or what is now Hungary]. . . . But through his [adopted] sons he could approach both situations on a parity, while keeping safe his majesty, for which the reverence was also greater because of distance. People would excuse young men referring certain issues to their father, and those resisting Germanicus and Drusus could be placated or coerced by him. But what other recourse was left, if they scorned the emperor? However, as though he were about to leave at any moment, he chose his entourage, readied his equipment, and fitted out ships. Then having cited variously winter or pressing matters of state, in the first instance, he duped those savvy politically, then the common people, and for the very longest time the provinces.

—TACITUS, *ANNALS* 1.47

Note how the use of these surrogates provided the emperor the ability to delay a decision or even to alter one without seeming to vacillate or risking his reputation for firmness. He reserved desperate measures for himself at the latest juncture. Tacitus observes that these ruses have staying power in inverse proportion to the proximity to the seat of power.

The emperor could also insulate himself from criticism in other ways. An emperor secure in his support could use the freedom to criticize as a means to enhance his own image. Pliny the Younger addresses the issue in his *Panegyric Oration,* an official speech of praise spoken in the senate on behalf of the emperor Trajan, who had recently come to power.

Thanks for Being Great Enough to Listen to Me Tell You How Great You Are

In fact nothing is satisfactorily praised without comparison, and, moreover, this is first duty for loyal citizens regarding the best emperor, that they attack those unlike him, for they cannot love good leaders enough who do not hate bad leaders enough. Add to the equation that no benefit of our emperor is broader or more pervasive than the fact that it is safe to attack bad leaders. . . . Therefore, in your case, Caesar [Trajan], I am making a comparison with all your services and I am rating above most of them that it is permitted both to avenge ourselves daily on the bad emperors in the past and to admonish by this example the future bad emperors.

—PLINY THE YOUNGER, *PANEGYRIC ORATION* 53.2–3, 5–6

We suspect that Pliny's advice would be especially well received in faculty senates around our country contemplating a new university president, or among boards of trustees appraising a new head football or basketball coach.

There is something that strikes the modern reader as not entirely sound in the psychology of obedience on which Pliny is trying to sell his audience. For one thing, how can people know that they are not being manipulated to criticize past rulers, and to give the incumbent a free pass? Nevertheless, freedom to criticize past regimes at least gives the illusion that the present leader is not above censure. It also implies almost subliminally that the reigning emperor must be free of the vices being condemned, because otherwise he would not allow such blame to be broadcast.

Networking

The Greeks and Romans knew they needed to scout out opportunities for pursuing professional goals by making contact with the people most likely to advance their interests. They formed collaborations through taking advantage of such contacts. Nowadays we have professional meetings, conventions, company open houses, and trade shows. Under the heading of networking, we have collected a series of anecdotes about mentorship and public relations.

In the ancient world, one could meet and impress large numbers of influential persons at the great international festivals, such as the religious celebrations to honor Olympian Zeus, held every four years. The Olympic festival, held at Olympia (in the city-state of Elis in southern Greece), was one of four ancient preeminent international religious occasions. It included the athletic contests on which our modern Olympics are modeled. The Greeks and later Romans believed intense competition strongly expressed proper reverence to Zeus and other gods. Protected by a military truce, the ancient games attracted a huge audience composed disproportionately of upper-class people. Not only was the journey to Olympia from distant regions of the Greek world expensive, but the competitors were also, for many centuries, primarily aristocratic. The demographics of the audience for international athletic competitions were rather like that for golf broadcasts on television.

The circuit of athletic games in various regions of Greece and the greater cycle of internationally renowned festivals were naturally venues in which the competitors and their aristocratic families and friends might relate to their social and

political peers from other states. These contacts had all sorts of important ramifications for economic and political relations. Such relationships were extended and publicized by the elaborate performances of choral lyric poems that were commissioned from internationally recognized poets and performed during the celebration of the return of the victorious athlete to his home city. The acknowledged master of such poetry was Pindar of Thebes, whose active career coincided with the first half of the fifth century B.C. Here, in his eighth Olympian victory ode for wrestling in the boys' division, he recalls the mentorship of an adolescent aristocrat from the island of Aigina by an aged Athenian champion, Melesias. Note that athletes from two cities could collaborate by means of the opportunity presented by international competition.

It's Who You Know!

To teach is easier for one who himself knows how, and the predisposition for such tutelage demonstrates intelligence, while the thoughts of the untested are rather trivial. Yet that master [Melesias] might explicate these endeavors beyond all others, especially what regimen will promote a man striving to win most coveted glory from the sacred games.

—PINDAR, *EIGHTH OLYMPIAN ODE* 54–66

Observe how the athletic instruction provided young Alcimedon by Melesias is part of a more general sponsorship in the appropriate comportment for a young member of the elite. The same kind of testing and tempering occurs today on teams (intercollegiate and intramural) at our elite colleges and in athletic clubs around the country.

It was not just athletes who took advantage of the Olympic festival to achieve their professional goals by networking with those persons most able to further their careers. Herodotus is considered to be "the father of history," a pioneer who established the methods of research essential to his profession. His subsequent written work rested on a foundation of oral presentations. How Herodotus expedited his inquiries and disseminated his initial findings is portrayed in the following account, which is derived from a discussion about the historian by Lucian, an author of the second century A.D. Lucian was particularly struck by this use of the Olympic Games.

And the "Word of Mouth" Was Dynamite!

[Traveling from Asia Minor] Herodotus considered how both he and his writings might become notable and renowned as quickly as possible and in the most trouble-free manner . . . [visits to various cities would involve delay] . . . Therefore, he decided not to disperse his effort nor to gather and collect a public response by audience segments little by little. But he planned (if it might be possible) to win all the Greeks together somewhere . . . [so he presented his work at the Olympic Games] . . . Immediately everyone knew of him better than even the Olympic victors themselves. And there was no one who had not heard the name of Herodotus, some hearing him themselves at Olympia and the rest learning from those returning from the festival. And if he showed up anywhere, people pointed him out.

—LUCIAN, *HERODOTUS* 1–2

Particularly striking here is the effort by Herodotus to achieve name recognition and an audience for his work through the most expeditious method that he could find. In this connection we might mention the tradition that the Athenians were so taken with his account of their contribution to the Greek victory over the Persians that they gave the historian a sizable monetary reward. The demographics of the ancient Olympic audience—we repeat—would have a modern account executive drooling over its affluence.

Everyone involved in business today doubtless appreciates the importance of occasions for interaction, like dinners, cocktail parties, happy hours, and even drinks with coworkers before heading home from work. Very early in the Western tradition, Greek poets were already extolling the symposium or drinking party as a means for attaining personal goals. Theognis is the name affixed to an important collection of aristocratic poetry that circulated among the inhabitants of the town of Megara in the sixth and fifth centuries B.C. During the height of Athenian democracy, these poems were also popular with upper-class Athenians.

The "Three-Martini" Symposium

You must know that these things are so. Do not associate with
    base men, but always stick to the noble gentlemen.
And drink and eat with them, and with them sit,
and win their favor, since their pragmatic ability is great.
You will learn good things from good men, but if you
associate with the base, you will in due course ruin what mind
    you have innately.
Learning these things, associate with the good, and one day you
    will say that I gave good advice to my friends.

—THEOGNIS, 1.31–38

Obviously, the ancient equivalent of hanging out with buddies to watch wrestling or Howard Stern was just as much a nonstarter for the young aristocrat inaugurating his career in the sixth century B.C. as it is for the young executive today. The negative example is clear from the reaction of the fourth-century historian Theopompus to the drinking parties with courtiers of his contemporary Philip II of Macedonia, the father of Alexander the Great.

Not Your Everyday Frat Pals; On Second Thought . . .

[Philip] praised and honored the extravagant and those spending their lives in dicing and drinking. . . . Some of them, although they were men, went about with bodies shaved and depilated, and others were ready to mount each other, although grown men with beards. And they brought around two or three boy-toys, and they themselves offered the same services as these to others. Thus someone would fairly consider them hookers instead of comrades, and address them rightly not as fellow soldiers but pushover sluts, because they were man killers by nature, and male whores by habit. Moreover, they loved to get drunk instead of staying sober, and, instead of living respectably, sought to rob and murder.

—THEOPOMPUS FRAGMENT 225

To a considerable degree, alcohol is still the drug most truly domesticated in our culture, and its status descends to us from the ancient Greeks. Determining how business contacts might behave in social settings was helpful in appraising their suitability for occupational and professional activities. Wine was a catalyst for the Greeks in reaching such judgments. Theognis is helpful once again.

Holding Your Booze Well!

Experts recognize gold and silver by fire,
but wine reveals the mind of a person,

even of a prudent man, who drinking beyond moderation
  buoys up
so that wine puts to shame even one who was wise before.

—THEOGNIS, 1.499–502

In the ancient world, public baths played the same role in networking that gyms, health spas, and country clubs perform in modern American society. They were casual environments for establishing relationships, and it was sometimes easier to get negotiations and the like consummated in such environments than elsewhere. These facilities were particularly numerous during the Roman Empire. One could even rub shoulders with the Roman emperor, as this amusing story shows. It is from the biography of Hadrian, a powerful and cultured leader, who reigned in the early second century A.D.

I'll Scratch Your Back, if . . .

Hadrian frequently bathed in public and with the common people, from which practice this bathing joke became famous. When he saw on a certain occasion a retired soldier known to him from his military service rubbing his back and the rest of his body on the wall, he asked why he gave himself to be rubbed down by marble walls. When he heard that this happened only because he had no slave, he presented the man with some slaves and resources for their upkeep. But on another day when many old men were rubbing themselves on the wall in order to stimulate the generosity of the emperor, he ordered them to be called out and each one to be rubbed down by another in turns.

—HISTORIA AUGUSTA, LIFE OF HADRIAN 17

Social connections among friends could lead to financial support in times of need. One way to raise money for a range of purposes was through what the Greeks called an *eranos* loan.

This was the loan of a sum of money (usually interest-free) to which friends subscribed. Such arrangements could of course be abused, and it is the nature of our evidence that we are best informed about cases where agreements were broken and could not be mended by the mediation of friends or arbitration, short of full litigation. One such story involves Apollodorus, a prominent and wealthy fourth-century Athenian whose father was a famous banker called Pasion. Some of his court speeches have been preserved among the surviving works of his great contemporary, the orator and statesman Demosthenes.

A friend and neighbor of Apollodorus named Nicostratus had gone in pursuit of some of his slaves who had run away, but had been captured by privateers and himself sold as a slave. Apollodorus had helped Nicostratus by supplying his brother with 300 drachmas of travel money to visit and redeem Nicostratus. We pick up our story as Nicostratus puts the touch on his friend, Apollodorus.

Loans Among Friends?

On his arrival home, Nicostratus came to me first, greeted me, and thanked me because I had provided travel money to his brother. And he lamented his misfortune, and accusing his own relatives he asked me to help him, just as I was formerly a true friend to him. Breaking into tears and telling me that he had been freed for 3,600 drachmas, he urged me to contribute something to his ransom. On hearing his story and pitying him, and seeing his bad condition . . . I answered that I had been a true friend in the past and I would help him in misfortune, and I freed him from the obligation of the 300 drachmas, and I answered that I would contribute an interest-free loan of 1,000 drachmas. . . . Not many days later, Nicostratus came crying to me that the foreigners who had lent his ransom were demanding the remainder back, and in his contract a thirty day period was established for repayment or a twofold amount was owed, and that no one wished to buy or mortgage the farm in my neighborhood. . . . He said, "Provide me with the remainder of the money before the thirty-day limit in order that the 1,000 drachmas already paid not be lost and I not be liable to seizure." "Collecting a friendly loan," he said, "when I send the foreigners on their way, I shall give you what you lend me."

—DEMOSTHENES, *AGAINST NICOSTRATUS* (53) 6–11

Rather than pay Apollodorus back, Nicostratus supposedly launched a harassment campaign against him, participating as a spy, witness, and coplaintiff in various legal actions in which Apollodorus was involved. If we can believe Apollodorus, Nicostratus even tried to throw him in a quarry late one night.

Losing Support

Modern observers must always be skeptical when historical figures claim that their popularity and ability to lead has been subverted by the moral degeneration of those led: Such claims often have the whiff of entitlement or ideological privilege about them. When Jimmy Carter found America pervaded by "malaise" in the midst of the failures of his administration, Americans preferred to change their leadership. Nevertheless, breakdowns in the common values of leaders and followers assume similar aspects then as now.

A lack of deference to the chain of command is character-istic of organizational breakdown. The early Greek poetry of Theognis provides a vivid presentation of the breakdown in the cooperation between leaders and followers. Theognis believed that his fellow citizens had turned against their city's traditional aristocratic leadership in favor of low-class and low-life infiltrators. In addition, economic vicissitudes and impoverishment had weakened the ability of our speaker to command deference and obedience.

Arranging Deck Chairs on the Titanic?

If I had my property, Simonides,
I would not be distressed as I am now at being together with
   the noble.
But now it has fled me, although I was alert, and I am mute
because of my poverty, although I am better aware than many
that we are now being carried along, with white sails lowered,
beyond the sea of Melos, through the dark night,
and they refuse to bail, and the sea washes over
both sides of the ship. It is a difficult thing for anyone
to be saved, such things they are doing. They have deposed
   the pilot,
that good man who was standing guard with expertise.
They seize possessions by force, and order has been destroyed.
There is no longer an equitable division, in the common
   interest,
but the passengers, merchandise carriers, rule, and the base are
   on top of the noble. I am afraid that perhaps a wave will
   swallow the ship.
Let these be enigmatic utterances hidden by me for the noble.
One could be aware of future misfortune, if one is wise.

—THEOGNIS, 1.667–682

Even if we are not entirely convinced by the poet, we can also take from him an unintended message. Beware the wrath of the genteel poor, that bane of managers in inherited firms.

Moreover, this passage is particularly noteworthy for its use of the "ship-of-state" metaphor, one of Greece's important gifts to our vocabulary of leadership. The political and social breakdown is therefore modeled on a merchant venture at sea that has dramatically gone bad.

Just as a following can become estranged from its chief, so too can a leader actively alienate his supporters. Accordingly, ancient writers also provide a useful catalog of the behaviors that stood the strongest chance of undermining one's support with followers. Self-indulgence and overt expression of divergence from values formerly shared could have a powerful self-subversive effect. The late Roman biographer Quintus Curtius Rufus gives a lurid account of how none other than Alexander the Great fell from grace with his Macedonian and Greek supporters in the 320s B.C.

Nothing Fails to Succeed Like Success

Yet, as soon as the mind of Alexander, more tolerant of military activities than of quiet and leisure, was freed from pressing concerns, indulgences seized him and vices conquered one whom the military might of the Persians had not broken, namely day-long banquets, an unhealthy gratification through drinking bouts and partying through the night, games, and crowds of sluts. Everything lapsed into an alien lifestyle, which Alexander emulated as though preferable to his own. In this way he so offended the eyes and hearts equally of his supporters that he was considered an enemy by many of his own friends. Indeed he impelled men who had clung fast to their own upbringing and were accustomed to enjoy a modest and accessible mode of life into the foreign evils of conquered peoples. Accordingly, conspiracies against his life were prepared more frequently, and mutiny of his soldiers and freer recrimination amid mutual complaints. And on Alexander's part there followed now rages, now suspicions that thoughtless fear aroused, and a catalog of similar faults.

—QUINTUS CURTIUS RUFUS, *HISTORY OF ALEXANDER* 6.2.1–4

Good leaders know how to take responsibility for problems. They do not try to divert blame, or, should we say, they

do so only at the risk of their credibility. The Roman emper-
or Nero attained considerable popularity early in his reign.
Not only did he favor excellent advisers, but his youth, physical presence, and good rapport with urban Romans stood
him in very good stead indeed. His reaction to adverse circumstances, however, did not contribute to his continued
standing and authority. In a famous passage, Tacitus describes
how Nero's cynical manipulation of public opinion backfired
when he abused the Christians after the great fire at Rome of
A.D. 64 (one of the most newsworthy events in antiquity and
the context for several of our examples). Nero had to act
when the rumor could not be squelched that he had ordered
the city set on fire.

How the Usual Suspects Got That Way

Therefore, for expunging the rumor Nero substituted as culprits and chastised with the most exquisite punishments persons, hated for their vices, whom the people called Christians.
The founder of the name, Christus, had been punished with the
death penalty by the procurator Pontius Pilate during the reign
of Tiberius, and this destructive superstition and cult, although
suppressed for the moment, broke forth again, not only in
Judaea, the source of the evil, but also in the city of Rome, to
which everything outrageous and disgusting flows and
becomes popular.

Arrests were made, and, after confessions, many Christians
were implicated and condemned on the charge of "hatred of
the human race." They were mocked, tortured, and executed
brutally.

Nero offered his gardens for this spectacle and presented a show
in the Circus Maximus, mixing with the common people in the
dress of a charioteer or mounted in his chariot. Then, regarding
these criminals who earned the most extreme novelties of pun-

ishment, compassion arose as though they were being destroyed not for public advantage, but for the savagery of a single man.

—TACITUS, *ANNALS* 15.44

Some managers can lose their way when they forget how they developed a constituency in the first place. Servius Sulpicius Galba was an old, distinguished Roman aristocrat who had compiled a highly esteemed military and administrative record in the early Roman Empire. When Nero's regime was descending into misadministration and irrationality, the seventy-two-year-old Galba had the courage to rise against the emperor. After Nero's suicide, Galba succeeded as emperor. He failed to realize, however, that the coalition supporting him was not universally composed of altruistic and public-spirited Romans. The empire was defended by a professional army, so that the soldiers, who were no longer ordinary citizens serving for terms, had become partners in government. This oversight was particularly problematic concerning the elite military units of the Praetorian Guard that were stationed at Rome itself. They were 9,000 strong and protected the emperor, his family, and the imperial administration. The guardsmen were accustomed to share in the important occasions of the emperor by receiving a cash gift.

Make Sure the New Year's Bonus Checks Are Cut on Time!

[Ominous weather] did not deter Galba from going to the camp of the Praetorian Guard . . . [announcing his adoption of a rather undistinguished noble youth as successor] . . . He added nothing to his oration, neither pandering nor a gift in payment. Nevertheless, the tribunes [officers] and centurions [noncommissioned officers] and the nearest of the soldiers responded with friendly attention. Among the rest of the soldiers, there was sullenness and silence, as though they had lost through the civil war the prerogative for a cash grant that had been usurped [on such occasions] in peacetime. It is generally believed that Galba would have been able to conciliate their feelings with even the slightest liberality on the part of a grudging old man. His old-fashioned stringency and excessive severity, to which we Romans are no longer equal, ruined his cause.

—TACITUS, *HISTORIES* 1.18

After the assassination of Galba in a mutiny of the Praetorian Guard, Tacitus ironically sums up his leadership style with a famous formulation: "while he was a private citizen, he seemed greater than a private citizen, and would have been considered capable of the imperial office by universal consensus *if he had not been emperor*" (*Histories* 1.48). In that age the "Peter principle" worked with a vengeance: rising above the level of your competence could leave you dead in the gutter like poor old Galba.

The Value of Theater: Is the Best Defense Always a Good Offense?

Success and sheer style of leadership can count for a lot, but it is also true that even an avowed master executive can lose his balance if he leaves himself without an exit strategy in management of his followers' moods. Let us then conclude this section with the case of Publius Cornelius Scipio Africanus, the great Roman general and statesman of the late third and early second centuries B.C. Scipio had conquered Spain, driving the Carthaginians from there, and he then invaded North Africa and defeated Hannibal decisively, giving the Romans victory in the Second Punic War. Scipio later collaborated with his brother in the Roman defeat of Antiochus III, who as a king of the Seleucid dynasty presided over most of the Middle East, a large portion of the former empire of Alexander the Great. Scipio's prestige was much resented by his political rivals, led by Cato the Censor, who was pushing a platform of traditional Roman values. Scipio was attacked by a tribune of the plebeians (an advocate of the common people), fronting for his political opponents, who made accusations about his and his brother's handling of funds in the war with Antiochus. Our source for the results is Polybius, a Greek historian and a friend of Scipio's grandson, who admired Scipio Africanus's greatness of character.

> Publius, being so great a seeker of honor under an aristocratic constitution, achieved such great admiration from the common people and trust with the senate that, when someone was demanding that he answer a charge before the people which was contrary to Roman tradition and accompanied by many bitter accusations, Publius said that it was not fitting for the people to hear any Roman denouncing Publius Cornelius Scipio, through whom those accusers had the very right and power of speaking at all. And most of those listening immediately dissolved the meeting in a group, leaving the accuser alone.
>
> —POLYBIUS, *HISTORIES* 23.14.1–4

This ploy made his accuser, the plebeian tribune, look rather petty. It did not hurt Scipio's cause that the charges were being made on the anniversary of Scipio's victory over Hannibal. Thus, he could change the day's "agenda" from answering his accusers to leading prayers to the gods for the past deliverance of Rome from its enemy.

Scipio had still another coup de théâtre to play.

We Do Not Recommend Trying This with the IRS

> Again, when someone was demanding an account in the senate of the money Africanus had taken from Antiochus before the treaty for paying his own troops, he said he had the account book, but that it was unnecessary for him to provide an

accounting to anyone. Yet, with his questioner pressing and bidding him to present the account book, he decided that his brother should provide it. When the book was brought in, holding it out before himself and tearing it up in the presence of the whole senate, he bade the man demanding it make an inquiry from the pieces. And he asked the other senators why they were looking into an account of 3,000 talents of silver, how it was spent and through whose agency, but that they were no longer investigating the total of 11,500 talents, which they had taken from Antiochus, how that sum came in and through whom, nor how they had become the masters of Asia, Africa, and Spain, with the end result that all the senators were not only struck into amazement, but even the man demanding the account fell silent.

—POLYBIUS, *HISTORIES* 23.14.1–11

This response did naturally forestall, at least for a time, the political enemies of Scipio. His performance was first-class political theater. Unfortunately, Scipio probably also forfeited the goodwill of many of his fellow senators with this arrogant posturing. Although it was, moreover, a dramatic gesture to rip up the account book, this coup also made it practically impossible to lay to rest definitively any suspicion that sums had indeed been embezzled—it is impossible to appeal to the records one has destroyed for their irrelevance. Scipio then decided to withdraw from public life and retire to a small villa, where he lived out his last few years. His historical reputation, however, was enhanced as the petty rivalries of his time receded into the past, and he achieved iconic stature for later Romans.

Our advice is to temper such magnificent theatricality with a little more self-deprecation. Yet it is true today that we have the advantage that ripping up our accounts does not preclude having copied them, with a set stored in a safety deposit box against the chance of a later audit.

3

Consulting and Decisionmaking

I f you hate meetings, then thank heavens that you did not live in classical Athens or (worse) Rome. And give further thanks even if you think your firm relies too much on external management consultants. For Greeks and Romans alike, in principle a leader was not supposed to make important decisions on any matter, private or public, without consulting family, friends, trusted associates, and sometimes even qualified strangers.

Well, that is in principle. In real life, we see that the ancients zigged and zagged on the question of best practices in solving problems and making decisions. Some leaders put a premium on surrounding themselves with trusted advisers who complemented their own strengths and weaknesses, and listened closely when these individuals spoke. Others only occasionally solicited conflicting points of view in their meetings. For them, the usual idea, it seems, was to cover their back in case things went horribly wrong. Finally, a few supremely self-confident characters dispensed with the tedium of deliberation and leaped into action without sounding out others' views.

"I Have a Friend . . . "

The fourth-century Greek orator, speechwriter, and pamphleteer Isocrates realized that folks have a certain squeamishness in asking for advice, especially when confidentiality is at stake. Here are some of his ground rules for sound and effective deliberations:

> In deliberating, make the past a precedent for the future; for the quickest way to discern the unknown is from what is known. Be slow in deliberation, but be quick in execution once you have decided. . . . Should there be matters about which you are ashamed to speak freely, yet wish to share with some of your friends, represent it as though it were another's affair. In this way you will get a sense of their opinion, and will not show your own hand. Whenever you intend to consult with anyone about your business, see first how he has managed his own. For he who has shown poor judgment in his own affairs will offer poor advice in that of others.
>
> —ISOCRATES TO DEMONICUS (1) 34–35

For the ancients, receiving and giving advice was a deeply ingrained habit. In Rome, even someone resolved on suicide might seek a committee's validation. After battling a three-month intestinal ailment at age seventy-seven, Cicero's close friend Atticus summoned his son-in-law and two close friends to his bedroom. Atticus then (unusually, for a Roman) told them up front that he was going to starve himself, and wanted no backtalk:

> Since I have, so I hope, satisfied you that I have done everything that is conducive to curing myself, what remains is for me to look after my own interests. I did not want to leave you in the dark about this: for I am resolved to stop nourishing the disease. . . . Therefore I beg of you two things, to approve of my

plan, and not to try to obstruct me by pointlessly advising me to the contrary.

—CORNELIUS NEPOS, *LIFE OF ATTICUS* 21.5–6

Consultants and Chutzpah

For senior management, the ancient world offered a bewildering choice of consultancy options. Oracle-mongers, soothsayers, prophets, priests—for their part, all eager to make a profit from other people's problems. In a real crisis, such individuals came out of the proverbial woodwork. Consider Thucydides' description of the mood at the outbreak of the Peloponnesian War between Sparta and Athens, and their respective allies in 431 B.C.:

> The Peloponnese and Athens each had plenty of young men who, out of inexperience, eagerly joined the war-effort. Meanwhile, all the rest of Greece was on tiptoes in anticipation at the conflict of the chief cities. In those cities preparing to fight—and elsewhere too—there was much reading of oracles, and much chanting by oracle-mongers.
>
> —THUCYDIDES, *THE PELOPONNESIAN WAR* 2.8.1–2

As a hedge against future complaints from their clients, professional consultants might keep their pronouncements open-ended.

> A charlatan prophet fell into the hands of the enemy, and disclosed that he was a seer, just as they

were about to fight a battle. "You'll defeat your foes," he pronounced, "provided that in the melée they don't see the hairs on
the backs of your heads."

—PHILOGELOS ("THE LOVER OF LAUGHTER") 205

That story, from a book of jokes published in late antiquity, is meant to be funny. However, a notorious example in this
very real genre of fuzzy predictions is the answer that two oracles—one of them Apollo's at Delphi—gave to ambassadors of
Croesus, king of Lydia (now western Turkey). Seeking encouragement for their master's plan to attack the growing Persian
empire of Cyrus the Great, envoys presented the oracles with
flashy gifts and then said:

> "Croesus, king of Lydia and other nations asks you whether he is
> to campaign against the Persians." That is what they asked, and
> the judgment of each of the two oracles concurred, foretelling
> that if Croesus should campaign against the Persians, he would
> destroy a great empire.

—HERODOTUS, *HISTORIES* 1.53 (ABRIDGED)

Well, Croesus's corporate raid on the Persian empire
failed miserably. His army defeated, the king was captured
and he narrowly missed being burned at the stake. When the
ashes settled, he sent envoys back to Delphi to complain.
But the priestess in charge of the oracle would not give the
Lydians a refund, saying that the defeated king had only
himself to blame:

> Apollo declared to Croesus, that if he campaigned against the
> Persians, he would destroy a great empire. If he intended to plan
> well, he ought to have sent and inquired which empire the god
> spoke of—that of Croesus or that of Cyrus.

—HERODOTUS, *HISTORIES* 1.91

Already in the latter half of the fourth century B.C.—almost two and a half millennia before the master of deliberate vagueness, Fed chairman Alan Greenspan—Aristotle could lay out the ABCs of indeterminate soothsayer-speak:

> Since speaking in general terms entails less risk of error, diviners speak generally about hard details. That's because in playing the game of "odd or even," you're more likely to be right if you say "even" or "odd" rather than a definite number. The same goes for saying "it will be," rather than "when."
>
> —ARISTOTLE, *RHETORIC* 1407B

When ancient consultants found themselves in hot water and lacked a way to climb back out, they sometimes simply resorted to chutzpah. Here again, from that late antique compendium of jokes, are some zingers directed at a stock character found in every period of antiquity:

> Someone approached a charlatan prophet and asked whether his enemy would return from a trip. The prophet said that he was not coming back. But when the man learned of his presence after a few days, the prophet rejoined, "How shameless can you get?"
>
> —PHILOGELOS ("THE LOVER OF LAUGHTER") 203

> On returning from a trip, someone approached a charlatan prophet and asked about his family. "They are all in good health," he replied, "especially your father." But the man said, "It's now ten years since my father's been dead!" The prophet answered, "See, you do not know your real father."
>
> —PHILOGELOS ("THE LOVER OF LAUGHTER") 201

By the way, like those oracles, savvy consultants were apparently notorious for getting their compensation up front:

An ill-tempered astrologer cast the horoscope of a sick boy, predicted to his mother that he would have a long life, and then demanded his fee. "I'll give it to you tomorrow," she answered. "But what happens," said the astrologer, "if he dies in the night? Am I to lose my payment?"

—PHILOGELOS ("THE LOVER OF LAUGHTER") 187B

Plainly, to put it in the language of Wall Street's financial analysts, that astrologer was a funny cross between a "bull" and a "bear." Every once in a while we see the shoe on the other foot. When Alexander the Great consulted Apollo's famous oracle at Delphi on his prospects in his war against Persia,

. . . and by chance arrived on one of the forbidden days, when it was deemed improper to deliver an oracle, he initially sent a messenger to call on the priestess. When she refused on the grounds of the law, Alexander went up himself and forcibly began to drag her into the shrine. The priestess, as if yielding to his urgency, said, "You are invincible, my son." When Alexander heard this, he declared he had no further need of another oracle, but had the response from her that he wanted.

—PLUTARCH, *LIFE OF ALEXANDER* 14.6–7

No one in antiquity tops Alexander when it comes to a coup de théâtre.

You Want the Truth?
You Can't Handle the Truth

Nicias the general was up against a wall. Sent by Athens in 415 B.C. to help implement a hostile takeover of Sicily during the Peloponnesian War, before long he ran into problems with unreliable suppliers. Trouble with troop recruitment and

morale dampened the general's spirits further, which prompted him to write a frank memo to the Athenians back home:

> I could have written to you different, more pleasant things than
> this, but certainly not more useful, if you need to deliberate
> with full knowledge of how matters lie here. At the same time,
> I understand your true natures. You wish to hear the most
> agreeable news, and later find fault if anything turns out for
> you to be different in result. Therefore I have thought it safer to
> disclose the truth.
>
> —THUCYDIDES, *THE PELOPONNESIAN WAR* 7.14.4

In an effort to dispense with sugar coating, that particular
general went a bit too far. Nicias never thought that his
Sicilian commission had much chance of success in the first
place; his primary object here seems not so much as to inform,
but to protect himself.

The ability to give genuinely disinterested, frank advice is
counted by Aristotle as a prime characteristic of the "great-
souled individual."

> He must be open both in hate and in love: concealment is the
> mark of a fearful man, and one who cares less for the truth
> than personal reputation. He must speak and act openly: he is
> outspoken on account of his contempt for other men, and can-
> did, save when he speaks with feigned self-deprecation, as he does
> to the masses.
>
> —ARISTOTLE, *NICOMACHEAN ETHICS* 1124B

But, as everyone knows, actually listening to such a guy
takes some self-control. Straight talk, however well inten-
tioned, can hurt. Sometimes it can rebound on the speaker.
Look what happened after the king of an antique City of Apes
suffered even a small dose of narcissistic damage. In one of the

fables attached to the collection by Aesop (a figure dated traditionally to the sixth century B.C.), two humans, one an
unflinching truth-teller and the other a pathological liar, had
stumbled into his domain; the Ape King commanded them to
be seized and brought before a full court, so he could inform
himself of the ways of homo sapiens. The liar, by extravagant-
ly flattering the king and his circle in human terms, won for
himself a valuable present. So the truthful traveler thought to
himself that honesty was not just the best policy—it might
earn him an even bigger reward.

> The King Ape turned to him and said, "You now, tell me.
> What do you think of me, and these whom you see before
> me?" Well, the inveterate truth-teller responded, "You are real-
> ly an ape, and all these are just as you are, and always will be:
> namely, apes." The King immediately gave the order to his court
> to mangle him with their teeth and claws, because he had spo-
> ken the truth.
>
> —AESOPICA 569

But let's escape from the planet of the apes to consider
Demaratus, the first Spartan king to win a victory at the
Olympic Games (chariot racing was his event). Deposed from
his kingship, he found himself in exile among the Persians—
indeed, as a member of the huge Persian army that was just
about to march against Greece for 480 B.C. King Xerxes summoned the exile and tried to pump him for information about
his homeland:

> "So tell me this: will the Greeks stand their ground, offering me
> battle? In my opinion, even if all the Greeks and everyone else in
> the west were mustered together, they are not battle-worthy
> enough to abide my attack, unless they are united. Nevertheless,
> I want to learn from you what you say about them."utu
> Demaratus asked in reply, "King, should I speak the truth to you

or what will be pleasing?" Xerxes ordered him to speak the truth. . . . "They will oppose you in battle," said Demaratus, ". . . whether there happens to be an army of a thousand men, or more than that, or less." When he heard this, Xerxes smiled and said, "What a strange thing you've said, Demaratus, that a thousand men would fight so great an army! . . . In these matters you are inexperienced and are talking a lot of nonsense."

—HERODOTUS, *HISTORIES* 7.101–103

Luckily for Demaratus, the Persian monarch showed himself far superior to the Ape King. He treated the Spartan's unpleasant advice as a bad joke and let him off scot-free. Unfortunately for Xerxes, Demaratus turned out to be right. The Greeks indeed stood up to the Persian forces, and defeated them soundly in a series of great battles.

The Athenians, for their part, got an earful of advice from the famous orator Demosthenes on the danger posed by Philip II of Macedon, father of Alexander the Great:

There is a certain safe-guard that the natural character of intelligent men possesses within itself. It provides benefit and safety to all, especially to democracies against tyrants. And what is it? Mistrust. Guard that, and don't let it go. You can come to no harm if you preserve it.

—DEMOSTHENES, *SECOND PHILIPPIC* (6) 24

For these sage words Demosthenes got lip service, but that is about all. The Athenians ignored his warnings, with the result that Philip systematically gained control of the whole of mainland Greece. Of course, the queen of unheeded advice was Cassandra, daughter of Priam, king of Troy. As the story goes, Apollo had promised to teach her the art of prophecy in return for sexual favors. Cassandra learned the art but then refused to let the god have his way; Apollo retaliated by depriving her prophecy of the power to persuade. This punishment had deadly consequences. When the Greeks left a hollow, troop-filled, high-rise wooden horse before the walls of Troy, Cassandra alone saw the "gift" for what it was, and predicted to the Trojans their own demise if it was brought within the walls. But people thought she was quite literally crazy. According to one late account, she was even locked up and guarded.

Many Heads Are Better Than One?

I know of only one way in which you can be sure you have done your best to make a wise decision. . . . You must get courageous men of strong views, and let them debate with each other.

So said Dwight Eisenhower—which, as noted, corresponds at least to the ancients' ideal of how to get good advice. Now, why exactly did they hold that as a principle? For a start, there was a strong feeling among the ancients that general opinion was more reliable than that of individuals:

It's possible that the multitude, though not individually composed of good men, nevertheless in coming together becomes better than its members—not as individuals but as a whole. Compare communal dinners, which are better than those supplied out of a single purse. For when there are many, each individual

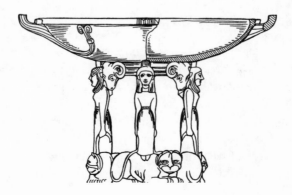

has a portion of virtue and good sense. And when they come together, just as the multitude becomes a single individual with many feet and many hands and possessing many senses, so also it becomes one individual in its moral disposition and intellect.

—ARISTOTLE, *POLITICS* 1281B

Put more succinctly:

In a group there is a certain great collective wisdom. Though its individual members may be deficient in judgment, the unit as a whole has much.

—PLINY THE YOUNGER, *LETTERS* 7.17.10

Or, in negative terms:

The opinion which is unsupported and isolated restricts its gaze to its own insight. But that which has gained the additional testimony of advisers serves as surety against error.

—ONASANDER, *THE GENERAL* 3.2

Thus Onasander, a Greek writing under Roman rule in the first century A.D., in his treatise on how to be a good commander. Yet among all those talking heads, the executive had to keep his own perspective.

The general must neither be so unstable in his judgment that he entirely distrusts himself, nor so obstinate as to think that nothing that another person has thought up is better than what he himself has. Inevitably such a man, either because he heeds everyone else and never himself, suffers numerous reverses, or else, because he virtually never listens to others but always to himself, makes many consequential mistakes.

—ONASANDER, *THE GENERAL* 3.3

In truth, the Greek didactic poet Hesiod—in a way, the Western world's first executive coach—was saying the same thing to his brother Perses around 700 B.C.

> Best of all is he who thinks over all things for himself,
> pondering what will be better for the future and at the end.
> And again, it is a good man who listens to a good adviser.
> But whoever neither thinks for himself nor takes to heart
> what he hears from another, that is a useless fellow.

—HESIOD, *WORKS AND DAYS* 293–297

Don't Stifle Debate

As the historian Herodotus tells it, when the Persian king Xerxes (486–465 B.C.) ran the most important meeting of his reign, he threw cold water on debate. Already resolved to launch a fresh expedition against Athens for 480 B.C.—one sent by his father, Darius, a decade before had ended in failure—Xerxes called together the top Persians and subordinate Greeks. His ostensible aim was to sound them out on his grandiose project of bridging the Hellespont and leading his army into Greece. The trouble was, he started by ruling out the possibility of U-turns before soliciting opinions. After Xerxes' brother-in-law Mardonius immediately jumped in praising the king as the wisest leader of the past, present, and future, the rest of the Persians (unsurprisingly) fell stone cold silent. But Artabanus, the king's uncle, piped up. Relying on his position, he said,

> King, if conflicting opinions are not voiced, it is impossible in
> making a choice to select the better: one must put into play
> what has been spoken. If they are voiced, it is possible to choose
> the better. In like manner we do not discern pure gold by itself,
> but when we rub it against other gold, we determine the better.

—HERODOTUS, *HISTORIES* 7.10 (ADAPTED)

By outlining all the risks inherent in such an enterprise, he made Xerxes question whether the expedition was such a good idea after all. Yet a new advisory service immediately stepped in. A heaven-sent vision of a tall, handsome man appeared to the king repeatedly in his sleep, and positively terrified him into pressing forward. Xerxes, in a controlled experiment, even made his nay-saying uncle sleep in his bed to confirm the dream. Artabanus saw the vision, too; in his case it seemed to threaten his eyes with hot pokers, which was quite enough to make him drop his resistance. But in this matter the gods who sent the vision turned out to be misleading consultants. The king lost much of his massive army and navy in Europe.

Little Help from One's "Friends"

Greeks thought themselves better than Persians at soliciting and taking advice. In the Hellenistic period (traditionally, 323–146 B.C.), every monarch maintained a highly structured council of "Friends" to aid in deliberations. So pity the poor Seleucid king Antiochus IV, who was all set to invade Egypt when a Roman envoy showed up carrying an unwelcome decree of the senate to cease hostilities. The Roman then intimidated Antiochus out of seeking advice in his customary manner:

> When the king, on reading it, said he wanted to communicate with his Friends about these circumstances, Popillius [the Roman ambassador] on hearing this acted in a way which seemed oppressive and extremely arrogant. He had at hand a stick cut from a vine, and with this vine-branch he drew a circle around Antiochus. He then ordered him to give his reply to the letter from within this circle. The king was astonished at what had happened, and at the overbearing attitude. But, after puzzling it over for a short time, he said he would do everything ordered by the Romans.
>
> —POLYBIUS, *HISTORIES* 9.27.4–6

Finding himself often too busy for consultative meetings, Julius Caesar thought up a way to make secure conference calls.

> It is said that Caesar first figured out how to communicate with friends by cipher, when, because of the volume of business and the great size of the city, a given occasion did not allow face to face conversation about urgent matters.
>
> —PLUTARCH, *LIFE OF CAESAR* 18.8

Isn't it ironic, then, that the punctilious Caesar missed out on the most famous piece of advice ever offered in antiquity? When he was offering sacrifice in early 44 B.C.,

> The soothsayer Spurinna warned him to beware of danger, which would come not later than the Ides of March.
>
> —SUETONIUS, *LIFE OF JULIUS CAESAR* 81.2

We all know what happened next.

Keep the Rubber Stamp Out of Reach

As Rome's emperors amassed ever more authority, they found it tougher to get honest feedback from what was supposed to be their chief advisory council, the Roman Senate. By chance, we possess on papyrus a speech by the emperor Claudius, where he takes the senate to task for being too quick to pass a motion exactly as drafted:

> Senators, if these proposals meet with your approval, indicate so at once, plainly and honestly. But if they are unsatisfactory, find another solution—yet do it here in this temple [the place of meeting]. Or if perchance you want to take the time to consider the matter more expansively, do so, provided that, in whatever order you are called, you remember that the opinion you

state must be your own. For, Senators, it is not in the least appropriate to the majesty of the senatorial class that one man alone, the consul designate [that is, the man traditionally first asked for his opinion], state his view here following the motion verbatim, and that the rest of you speak merely one word, "I agree," and then on leaving say, "We *did* speak."

—CLAUDIUS, FROM THE BERLIN COLLECTION OF GREEK
DOCUMENTARY PAPYRI, 611 COLUMN 3.10–22

In truth, by Claudius's day, Roman emperors had long been transacting the real business of the state in a sort of "executive committee." It was Augustus, the first Roman emperor (27 B.C.-A.D. 14), who institutionalized the notion of a "consilium" or privy council. He took as advisers a cross section of senators and chief magistrates, and used them to sound out important matters before floating them before the senate as a whole. As emperor of Rome, Marcus Aurelius (A.D. 161–180) took his privy council quite seriously. Found among his favorite sayings is this:

It is more just that I should follow the advice of my friends, who are so many and so prominent, than that my many, prominent friends should follow my individual will.

—MARCUS AURELIUS, *SAYINGS* 5

You have to be careful, however, as to the "friends" whose advice you seem to be taking. A CEO who decides to stock the company's board of directors with golf partners and family relatives should have a thick skin, for people will mutter. In antiquity, too, an executive's reputation was tied to that of his advisers. For instance, not long after seventeen-year-old Nero took up the Roman throne in A.D. 54, the Parthians, who controlled Mesopotamia (and the lucrative trade routes that passed through it) precipitated a crisis in the east by ravaging

Armenia. The chattering classes used this as an opportunity to speculate on how the new emperor and his predecessor Claudius—or more precisely, their respective advisory boards—would compare. Would Nero's people recommend the best commander for the job at hand, or someone from the old-boy network of the previous regime?

> At the top, things generally were managed through legitimate authority and structured deliberations more than by the sword and hand. The emperor would plainly show whether he was advised by good or bad friends, if he would put aside all jealousy and pick some eminent commander, rather than select a rich man who relied on his personal influence and campaigned for the position.
>
> —TACITUS, *ANNALS* 13.6

To the delight—and surprise—of the senate, Nero chose an experienced military man to secure Armenia.

With Age Comes Wisdom

For consultants, alleges the Roman poet Horace, technical expertise is not strictly necessary:

> I will function as a whetstone, which can make steel sharp, though itself not capable of cutting.
>
> —HORACE, *ART OF POETRY* 304–305

Age and experience are what really counted. To get good advice, a rule of thumb was to garnish one's council with at least a few folks of equal or senior status. As Homer's Menelaus points out in the *Iliad*:

The hearts of younger men are always unstable.
But in whatsoever an old man has a share, he looks both for-
    ward and back
so that it may turn out by far the best on both sides.

—HOMER, *ILIAD* 3.108–110

More fully the wise adviser par excellence, Nestor, com-
pared himself to the hero Diomedes, treating the same theme
more fully:

"you are very mighty in battle,
and in counsel you are best among all your contemporaries.
No one out of all the Achaeans will scorn your word
nor speak against it. Yet you have not reached the culmination
    of words.
You are truly young! You might even be my son,
the youngest in birth. Yet you address prudent thoughts
to the kings of the Argives, since you have spoken properly.
But let me who boasts that he is older than you
speak forth and expose the whole issue. And no one
will dishonor my remarks, not even lord Agamemnon.

—HOMER, *ILIAD* 9.52–62

That is why Sparta called its top public council the
Gerousia, from the same root as *geriatric.* Rome, of course, had
its senate, occupied (originally) by senior ex-magistrates.

If you can't get your hands on the wise, make sure that the
board at least excludes the disreputable. The Roman emper-
or Alexander Severus (A.D. 222–235) was thought unusual
for assembling and maintaining an upstanding group of
councillors:

Not malicious men, nor thieves, nor factious, nor cunning, nor
determined on doing evil, nor hostile to the upright, nor slaves

to their passions, nor cruel, nor active behind the emperor's
back, nor contemptuous, nor the type of men that considered
him to be sort of an idiot.

—*HISTORIA AUGUSTA, LIFE OF ALEXANDER SEVERUS* 66.2

This is a laundry list, one supposes, of the type of individuals who usually filled directors' chairs in that era. Much earlier, in 70 B.C., Cicero assailed one governor of Sicily, the corrupt Gaius Verres, for actively scraping the bottom of the
barrel to form an advisory council for trials:

What men constitute that retinue? Volusius the soothsayer,
and Cornelius the physician [for the Romans, a low-status
occupation], and these dogs whom you see licking the judg-
ment-tribunal.

—CICERO, *VERRINE ORATIONS* 2.3.28

Keep Your Decision Process Transparent

At least Verres paid lip service to transparency in his decisionmaking. There was a nasty rumor afloat that Cicero, while
holding Rome's chief magistracy in 63 B.C., in his home with
his wife, privately held trials of revolutionary followers of the
renegade politician Catiline (Pseudo-Sallust, *Invective Against
Cicero* 3). The historian Tacitus tells a similar story of the
emperor Claudius as if it were fact. An unusually distinguished
public man, the wealthy Valerius Asiaticus had landed himself
in hot water with the court in A.D. 47.

No trial before the Senate was granted him. It was conducted in
the emperor's bedchamber, in the presence of [empress]
Messalina. There [the prosecutor] Suilius accused him of cor-
rupting the troops, of binding them with bribes and a laissez-
faire attitude toward their sexual activities to share in every

crime, then he made the charge of adultery with Poppaea [a famous beauty, detested by Messalina], and finally of being an effeminate homosexual. At this last item, the defendant broke his silence. "Suilius, ask your own sons: they will confess that I am a man."

—TACITUS, *ANNALS* 11.2

The upshot? Poppaea committed suicide, shortly followed by Asiaticus, who took pains to ensure that his demise was environmentally responsible. When he saw that his funeral pyre was being prepared in a spot that might damage some leafy trees, he ordered it moved as his last act before suicide.

Tyrants Out of Touch

The advice of advisory councils was in principle nonbinding. It took some self-assurance to go against the grain and reject a majority opinion, but it was perfectly legitimate to do so. Far different was to make life-and-death decisions without any consultation, entirely on one's own initiative. That is said to have been one of the hallmarks of Tarquin the Proud (traditionally, 534–510 B.C.), the last of the seven Roman kings, before the founding of the Republic in 510 B.C. Having usurped the throne in Rome, it is said he consciously cultivated an arrogant management style. He assembled a bodyguard, which raised a few eyebrows. But it was in his dealings with the senate where Tarquin broke most completely with the precedents set by his six predecessors.

It got to the point where, since he had no hope of warming the hearts of the citizens, he had to maintain his kingdom by fear. To terrify effectively his subjects, he conducted trials for capital cases without the presence of advisers. In this way he was able to put to death, exile, or fine not only those whom he suspected or hated, but also those from whom the only thing he could

expect was material gain. . . . He was the first of the kings who
dispensed with the traditional custom of consulting the Senate
on all matters, the first who administered the government on
the advice of his personal intimates. He made or unmade war,
peace, treaties, alliances, just as he wished, without any authority from either People or Senate.

—LIVY, *HISTORY OF ROME* 1.49.4–5, 7

Not coincidentally, Tarquin the Proud was to be over-
thrown by a popular revolt, and the old-style monarchy gave
way to a new rationalized system of government centered on
two "consuls" of equal power, each with the capability of
vetoing the other, and holding office for just one year.

Arrogant, autocratic behavior also characterized the
Roman rebel governor Sertorius's descent into despotism.
Losing control of the troops and allies who had helped him
hold out in Spain for so many years (approximately 82–72
B.C.), it is said:

He conducted capital cases without a council or advisers; in private he heard the evidence, and appointing himself sole judge,
pronounced the sentences. He did not deign to invite his commanders to his banquets, nor did he bestow courtesies on his
friends. In general, because his position was steadily growing
worse, Sertorius turned into a beast and behaved like a tyrant
toward everyone.

—DIODORUS THE SICILIAN,
LIBRARY OF UNIVERSAL HISTORY 37.22A

That's not too far off from what psychologists call "projec-
tion." This particular tyrant fell victim to a boardroom coup:
his most trusted advisers invited him to dinner, where he got
the dagger treatment.

When It's Time to Decide

Aristotle, for one, had a keen sense of when it was time to move toward calling a meeting to a close:

> When we know a thing, and we have made our decision, there is no need of further words.
>
> —ARISTOTLE, *RHETORIC* 1391B

Sometimes, however, it's not good to pound the gavel too quickly. Serious matters require mature consideration, as Athenian ambassadors point out to an assembly in Sparta contemplating war against their city in 432 B.C.:

> Do not be hasty, then, in your deliberations, since they do not concern trivialities. And do not bring on domestic trouble, having been persuaded by outsiders' opinions and complaints. Do closely consider how great is the irrational element in war, before you are in the midst of it. For war, as it drags on, generally turns into a series of accidents, from which one of us is no more removed than the other, and whose result we risk in uncertainty.
>
> —THUCYDIDES, *THE PELOPONNESIAN WAR* 1.78.1–2

As it happened, the Spartans and their allies took those chances. They embarked on the Peloponnesian War (431–404 B.C.), which—after lots of thrills and spills—they managed to win, in no small measure thanks to help from Persia. For their part, the Persians are said to have developed a system to keep themselves from jumping into ill-considered schemes. According to Herodotus:

> They are in the habit of deliberating about the most serious issues when they are drunk. What they resolve in their counsels, this the master of the house where they deliberate proposes to

them on the following day. And if they still approve of it when sober, they put it into effect, but if they do not approve of it, they let it go. And if they have first deliberated about a matter when sober, they vote on it again when they are drunk.

—HERODOTUS, *HISTORIES* 1.133

Once you've investigated, debated (both drunk and sober, if that's your custom), and decided on a particular alternative, you'd better make sure it's practicable. Here the rodent world has a famous lesson to offer:

The Mice once held a council to see how they could protect themselves from a Cat. One wise mouse said, "Let's tie a tiny bell on the Cat's neck, and then we'll be able to hear him whenever he comes this way and be on guard for his traps." All approved of this plan. But when one mouse asked, "Who will tie the bell onto the Cat?" another said, "I'm not doing it." Still another said, "I wouldn't want to get so close to him for the whole world."

—AESOPICA 613

The philosopher Pythagoras put the final decision of that meeting more briefly, it is said.

Do that which will not harm you, and think before you act.

—PYTHAGORAS, *GOLDEN POEM* 39

Taking Action

Take counsel before you begin, and once you have deliberated, you need to act promptly.

—SALLUST, *CATILINE* 1.6

So writes the Roman historian Sallust, in the "philosophy lite" preface to his study of the insurgent Roman noble Catiline, who tried to get various dissident elements to rise in revolution in 63 B.C. when he found himself shut out in his third attempt at the consulship, Republican Rome's highest office. One of Catiline's leading followers, a certain Cethegus, is said to have taken a different view. During the preparations for the grand uprising, he complained:

> His associates by hesitation and procrastination were wasting big opportunities. In such a dangerous enterprise one needs action, not planning. If a few were to help, though the rest were faint of heart, he would attack the Senate-house.
>
> —SALLUST, *CATILINE* 43.3

Sallust means to characterize that man as a hot-headed fool. Yet the Stoic philosopher Epictetus (late first and early second century A.D.) also emphasizes the need for speed, albeit after proper reflection. You should act boldly, in full confidence, so long as you think you have right on your side:

> When you have decided that something must be done, and you are doing it, never shrink from being seen in the process, even if the masses are likely to form a mistaken impression of it. For if you are not acting rightly, shrink from the act itself. If rightly, however, why are you afraid of those who incorrectly have chastened you?
>
> —EPICTETUS, *HANDBOOK* 35

What happens if you aren't acting correctly, and know it? Well, here Cicero's letters to his brother Quintus (governor of the Roman province of Asia Minor 61–59 B.C.) offer some examples of stern fraternal advice:

You must not consult the opinions and judgments of merely the present generation, but also those of future people. And yet posterity's judgment, freed of detraction and malice, will be the more genuine.

—CICERO, *LETTERS TO HIS BROTHER QUINTUS* 1.1.43

A high standard, indeed. But Cicero elsewhere acknowledges that U-turns are possible, indeed blameless:

Never has a well-informed man . . . said that it was fickleness to change a plan.

—CICERO, *LETTERS TO ATTICUS* 16.7.3

Others begged to differ, the late fifth-century Athenian orator Antiphon among them. In some cases, there was no other course than full steam ahead.

In a matter that can be undone, it's a less serious error to give in to one's anger and be swayed by prejudice: you could still change your mind and arrive at the right decision. However, in situations where things can't be undone, changing your mind and recognizing that you have erred adds to the damage done.

—ANTIPHON, *ON THE MURDER OF HERODES* (5) 91

For charlatan prophets, dodgy soothsayers, and oracle-mongers, that second bit will not have come as news. But by then, they have usually collected their fees.

4

Strategy

K nowing what you want is one thing. But how to get it? And maintain it? In essence, this is the science of strategic planning. And an elaborate science it is. Clearly, it is no accident that the field of corporate strategy has spawned (among other things) much of modern business-speak—especially of the more euphemistic sort. In recent years, phrases such as "core competencies," "market segmentation," "vertical integration," and "competitive advantage" have become commonplace terms, cropping up far from the business schools where they were born.

Most of the main themes in the subdiscipline of strategy have ancient roots. In particular, if you're in the habit of talking about strategic management in military lingo, you're part of a long historical tradition. After all, Greek *strategia* means generalship or the skills of a commander, just as *strategemata* are individual pieces of generalship. The Roman technocrat Frontinus, writing at the start of the second century A.D., explains the difference between the two:

> Everything a leader achieves thanks to foresight, advantage, excellence, or determination, will be reckoned as "strategy." Actions

that fall under a particular type of these attributes will be counted as "stratagems." The characteristic power of stratagems, resting
as it does on skill and cleverness, is effective just as much when
one must evade the enemy as when one must crush him.

—FRONTINUS, STRATAGEMS 1 PREFACE

Another ancient military writer chimes in, expanding on
the importance of enterprise as a component of strategy. In
the preface to a volume of *Stratagems* dedicated to the Roman
coemperors Marcus Aurelius and Lucius Verus, he insists:

Clever generals show the foremost wisdom by winning a victory that involves no peril. Best of all is to devise amid the very
melée a way in which one's judgment can bring about the
means of winning, anticipating the outcome of the battle.

—POLYAENUS, STRATEGEMS 1 PREFACE 3

In Thucydides' *History of the Peloponnesian War,* the Spartan
general Brasidas expands on the same idea. Explaining his plan
to send just a portion of his army to surprise a careless
Athenian force, he says:

The person most likely to succeed is he who best sees this type of
blunder on the part of the enemy and, as his resources permit
him, makes an attack—not openly and in formation, but in
whatever way is expedient in the present situation. For the stratagems by which you can especially deceive the enemy and benefit your friends to the greatest degree are the ones that have the
best reputation.

—THUCYDIDES, THE PELOPONNESIAN WAR 5.9.4–5

But it is ancient Egypt that provides the first extended strategy lesson in this chapter. This case study comes from a time

when a Macedonian dynasty, the Ptolemies, was nearing the end of its domination of that fantastically wealthy country, a period of rule that lasted almost three centuries (323–31 B.C.).

Cleopatra Recapitalizes Her Firm

You've got to hand it to the dynasty of the Ptolemies. Founded by a general of Alexander the Great, this Hellenistic powerhouse always kept its eye on the prize when it came to resource development and renewal. Granted, some of their royal strategies come off as perverse: brother-sister marriage, for one. Others seem a mite obsessive. For instance, to control the wealth of Egypt, they set up an elaborate system of state monopolies, vertically integrating just about every process down the value chain. External wars and internecine conflict gradually took their toll on the Ptolemies, and by the first century B.C. their dynasty had degenerated into a fragile joke. But Queen Cleopatra VII, last of the Ptolemies, was to remind everyone that when a firm is going belly up, it is not the time to take half measures.

Badly needing financial support in 41 B.C., Cleopatra decided to center her recapitalization strategy on a certain Marc Antony, who at the time was reorganizing the eastern portion of Rome's territorial empire. But she didn't come begging. Rather, biding her time around Tarsus (in southwest Turkey, near the border with Syria),

> She received many letters, both from Antony and from his friends, summoning her. But as if in contempt and mockery of the man, she sailed up the river Cydnus in a golden-sterned barge, its purple sails unfurled, rowed by silver oars in time to flute-music, accompanied by Pan's pipe and lyres. Cleopatra herself reclined under a woven gold canopy, adorned like Venus in a picture, and young boys, made up to look like picture-book Cupids, stood on each side and fanned her. Likewise the most beautiful of her handmaidens wore the garb of sea nymphs and

Graces, and some were placed at the helm, others at the ropes. Wonderous scents from fragrances spread from the ship over the river banks.

—PLUTARCH, *LIFE OF ANTONY* 26.1–4

By the way, we are told that Cleopatra's actual beauty was not so remarkable. Rather, it was her charm, charisma, conversation, and facility with foreign languages (she was one of the few Ptolemies who took the trouble to learn Egyptian) that made her so attractive—not to mention her sense of theatricality. Cleopatra's bit of theater at Tarsus was a stratagem (that is, a short-term plan) driven by a long-term strategy. To cut to the chase, Antony spent the following winter with Cleopatra in Egypt; twins were soon born to the couple. But the liason was to prove a real strategic disadvantage for Antony over the decade that followed. In 30 B.C. the couple was dead, their rival Octavian (the future Roman emperor Augustus) supreme.

Hedge Your Bets

When a triumphant Octavian returned to Rome after finally defeating Marc Antony, among the well-wishers was a man holding a raven, which he had trained to say: "Hail, Caesar, victorious leader." Octavian was amazed at this courteous bird, and bought him at a handsome price. Yet the trainer's partner, who had received nothing from that generous payment, revealed to Octavian that the trainer had also a second raven, and requested that he be forced to produce it. Once it was fetched, the raven spoke the words it had learned: "Hail, Antony, victorious leader." Octavian was not at all irritated; he simply thought it enough to make the trainer split the money with his associate.

—MACROBIUS, *SATURNALIA* 2.4.29

The outcome could have been a lot worse. Indeed, it was only chance (and greed) that prevented the bird trainer's strategy from paying off 100 percent. Xerxes' uncle Artabanus would have sympathized. In the context of the Persian deliberations of the late 480s B.C. on whether to invade Greece, according to the historian Herodotus, he said:

> I find that there is the greatest profit in a well-laid plan. For even if later something stands in its way, what was planned remains just as good, and it is by chance that the plan was undone. But the individual who has planned poorly, if chance favors him, then he has lighted upon a windfall, and what he planned is no less bad.
>
> —HERODOTUS, *HISTORIES* 7.10B

But a corollary comes to mind. If your strategy is stupid from the start, and it turns out badly, then you deserve whatever you get. Look what happens when an actual member of the crow family tries to make a foray into new, highly competitive territory, without first drawing up a revamping plan in the event of a setback:

> A jackdaw who was superior in size to other jackdaws looked down on his peers and migrated to the crows; he thought it a good idea to live with them. But not recognizing his size and voice, they physically beat him and sent him packing. Once expelled by the crows, he returned to the jackdaws. But they didn't accept him, for they were angry at his presumption. So it happened that the jackdaw was deprived of association with both.
>
> —AESOP, *FABLES* 201

Define Yourself, Define Your Objectives

Before committing himself to this risky strategy, it might have helped if the ambitious jackdaw first made an internal analysis of his asset mix. In this passage from Xenophon's *Socratic Memoirs,* Socrates (put to death at Athens in 399 B.C.) shares his thoughts on leadership skills, "the kind of excellence through which men become good statesmen and managers, capable of ruling, and useful to mankind as well as themselves ... the noblest kind of excellence, the greatest skill, for it is the mark of kings and is deemed 'kingly.' He then continues:

Those who do not know and are self-deluded as to their capabilities ... know neither what they want, nor what they are doing, nor with whom they are dealing. Mistaken in all these respects, they fall short of the good and fall into the bad. Those who know what they are doing, get the object of their business and win a good reputation and honors. Their peers are delighted to deal with them, and those who are unsuccessful in their business want them to offer advice on their affairs, take them as their leaders, and rest on them their hopes of good things to come, and for all these reasons are fond of them above all other men. . . . In the case of communities, you see that whatever states, in ignorance of their own power, take stronger peoples to war, some are laid to waste, while others become slaves instead of free.

—XENOPHON, *SOCRATIC MEMOIRS* 4.2.11, 27–29

Or to put that extended thought in the language of Delphi, the Greek world's foremost oracle, "know thyself." That phrase was one of two carved above the door of Apollo's temple at the site. The other was "nothing in excess." For trying to turn the latter adage into a successful model for management, it would be hard to match the Roman emperor Antoninus Pius (A.D. 138–161), at least as portrayed by his adopted son Marcus Aurelius (ruled 161–180):

From my father I learned mildness, tranquil constancy in decisions taken after close examination, lack of vain conceit in so-called honors, a love of hard work, and endurance. Furthermore, the willingness to listen to those having something to propose for the common good, the habit of strictly apportioning to each man as he deserved, and the know-how as to when there was need for exertion or for relaxation. . . . His character had no aspect that was harsh, nor inexorable, nor violent, nor, as the saying goes, "carried to the sweating point." But he examined all things individually, as if he were at leisure, and in a steady, systematic way, vigorously and consistently.

—MARCUS AURELIUS, *MEDITATIONS* 1 16.1, 9

Know Your Competition

Yet the type of self-study urged by Socrates, Marcus Aurelius, and Delphi is just step one for the business manager. Step two is analyzing the competition. Here warfare teaches the sterner lessons:

What does a good general need to know and be able to do? . . . First, he must have the capability of recognizing against whom to make war, and with what allies. For this is the foundation of strategy. If one goes wrong here, what necessarily follows is a war which is disadvantageous, difficult, and superfluous.

—ISOCRATES, *ANTIDOSIS* (15) 117

When sizing up antagonists, it's particularly important not to leap to unwarranted conclusions. Certainly don't be like the butt of this mossy old joke on jumping too quickly to judgment.

A moronic elementary school teacher suddenly glanced at the corner of the class and shouted, "Dionysius is out of line in the corner!" When some one commented that Dionysius was not yet present, the teacher answered, "Well, he'll be out of line when he gets here!"

—PHILOGELOS ("THE LOVER OF LAUGHTER") 61

Of course, articulating a strategy and then implementing that plan is its own form of education. Xenophon praises a fourth-century Spartan king for being better than

a man who chances upon a treasure, who would become wealthier but not at all wiser in business. Or the man who wins a victory after an epidemic has hit his enemy, who would be more successful, but not in the least better at strategy.

—XENOPHON, *LIFE OF AGESILAUS* 10.1

It's telling that Xenophon can speak of business and army strategy in the same breath. For the ancients, as for moderns, the two domains probably did not seem all that remote.

Strike While the Iron Is Hot

Thanks to ancient compilers, a lot of stratagems have come down to us, attached to many of the most famous military men (and some women) of antiquity. If you want genuinely sleazy business tricks, well, the fourth century B.C. was a veritable golden age. Take this story about Iphicrates, a famous Athenian general of the period, who in a sting operation anticipated the entrapment methods of RICO enforcement in the United States:

He once fitted out his own fleet in the enemy's manner, and sailed to a people he viewed with suspicion. When they welcomed him effusively and enthusiastically, he sacked their town, now that he had unmasked their treason.

—FRONTINUS, *STRATAGEMS* 4.7.23

Descriptions of long-term strategies, however, are relatively rare in ancient sources. Thucydides provides perhaps the most memorable, in his sketch of how Pericles urged the Athenians to wage the Peloponnesian War. He convinced them to bring within the walls their property from the vulnerable countryside, and themselves to come into the city and guard it. If wealthy Athens kept its focus on wearing down Sparta by attrition, it would win the war.

> He said that if they kept quiet, paid attention to the fleet, did not extend the empire while engaged in war, and did not expose the city to risk, they would prevail. But what they did was the total opposite. Prompted by private political ambitions and private business interests, they put their hand to affairs that seemed quite external to the war, in a manner ruinous both to themselves and to their allies. These affairs, if successful, entailed honor and advantage more for private citizens, but if they failed, damaged the city for the conduct of the war.
>
> —THUCYDIDES, *THE PELOPONNESIAN WAR* 2.65.7

In other words, when times are so tough that you've reconsolidated your firm by closing your branch offices, it's probably not a good time to commit reserve capital to high-yield but high-risk ventures.

Sustaining a Competitive Advantage

So Pericles' successors did the opposite of what he had advised them, with results to match. But sometimes even good management can yield disappointing outcomes. Sustaining success is a dynamic process—one all too rarely seen, according to the later Athenian orator Demosthenes:

> Most men acquire wealth by planning well and disdaining nothing. But they do not care to preserve it by the same means.
>
> —DEMOSTHENES, *AGAINST LEPTINES* (20) 50

Here the consummate manager Cyrus, founder of the Persian empire, shares some golden wisdom on the same topic with rich king Croesus of Lydia (in the western part of modern Turkey). As we have seen, Cyrus had defeated Croesus in battle in 560 B.C. and almost burned him to death at the stake, but was prompted by a variety of factors (human and divine) to spare the Lydian and employ him as a wise adviser. Cyrus does not count as truly happy those who have and guard the most,

> for if that were the case, those would be happiest who guard the city walls. For they protect everything in the city. But whoever can in righteousness acquire the most and virtuously use the most—he is the person I consider most happy.
>
> —XENOPHON, *EDUCATION OF CYRUS* 8.2.23

It took Aristotle to break these basic, common sentiments down into quality objectives:

> There are four attributes which the head of a household must have to deal with his property. First, the ability to acquire. Second, the ability to preserve what is acquired: if he doesn't have that, there is no benefit in acquiring. It's as good as baling bilge-water with a colander, or the proverbial wine-jar that sports a hole. Third, he must know how to improve his property. Fourth, how to make use of it. After all, those latter two attributes are why we want the ability to acquire and preserve.
>
> —ARISTOTLE, *ECONOMICS* 1344B

The Original Pyrrhic Victories

As for the manager "preserving what he has acquired," King Pyrrhus could have taken a page from Aristotle's book. Invading Italy from his kingdom of Epirus (the northwest of Greece), he held out against the Romans for six years (276–270 B.C.), winning the battles but losing the war. The heavy casualties he sustained have made the expression "Pyrrhic victory" proverbial: In his alleged words, "one more such victory over the Romans and we are utterly undone." Pyrrhus was an experienced, courageous, enterprising leader. A pity he came up short in the strategy development department:

> What he gained by his exploits he quickly lost again by misplaced hopes, and by yearning for what was out of reach, he kept nothing of what was at hand. So Antigonus [another Hellenistic monarch] used to compare him to a player with dice, who had many superb throws, but did not know how to use them once they fell.
>
> —PLUTARCH, *LIFE OF PYRRHUS* 26.1–2

Hannibal and the Cannibal

The Carthaginian military leader Hannibal allegedly heard something similar from one of his subordinate officers:

> You know how to win a victory, but you do not know how to use it.
>
> —PLUTARCH, *LIFE OF FABIUS* 17

The context? Just halfway through the Second Punic War, in difficult—but hardly insuperable—circumstances, Hannibal let his strategic sense almost entirely desert him. When the major city of Capua in south Italy came back under Roman control (211 B.C.), other Italian towns naturally considered switching their allegiance from Carthage back to Rome. Hannibal knew it was military suicide to divide his army to keep watch on all the far-flung places in question. But his attempt at damage control ignited new flames of resentment:

> With some cities he allowed himself even to go back on his treaties, transplanting their populations to other cities, and open-

ing up their livelihoods to plunder. People took offence at this, and accused him of impiety or savagery. For these actions went hand in hand with robbery of money, murders, and pretexts for violence, perpetrated by both the outgoing or incoming soldiers in the cities, because they supposed that the inhabitants that were left behind were on the brink of crossing over to the enemy.

—POLYBIUS, *HISTORIES* 9.26.7–9

In other words, the Carthaginian soldiers were like the moronic schoolteacher's take on little Dionysius the schoolboy: leaping to conclusions. Then again, Hannibal himself when strategizing was a little tone deaf to human considerations. Let's turn back the clock some eight years, when the Carthaginian general was planning the march from Spain and then across the Alps to invade Italy. The main snag for him was the problem of providing food and securing provisions for his army in hostile country.

It appears that at that time this subject came before the council on multiple occasions. When no solution presented itself, one of his friends—Hannibal the Gladiator—pronounced it as his opinion that there was but one road open to him by which he could make it to Italy. When bidden to explain what it was, he said that they must teach the forces to eat human flesh, and make them used to it. Hannibal himself was able to say nothing against the boldness and efficacy of the notion, but was unable to persuade himself or his friends to contemplate implementing it.

—POLYBIUS, *HISTORIES* 9.24.5–7

Hannibal should have sacked his friend on the spot. This guy, Mr. Gladiator, was to perpetrate all sorts of loathsome acts in Italy that became attached to the reputation of Hannibal himself. Lesson: When one of your key executives is a cannibal, don't be surprised when your brand becomes a turn-off for customers.

5

Competition

Competition was a basic feature of existence then as now; commonly competition over fertile land became a cause for war. In the beginning of the development of Greek economic life, concepts of private ownership, competition, and individualism evolved in conjunction with each other. At the end of the Dark Age and the very beginnings of the period of literacy, Hesiod was a master poet in a tradition of rural poetry and advice that existed in central Greece during the eighth and seventh centuries B.C. His *Works and Days* is a compendium of wisdom of the nonaristocratic farmers of that age. In this passage, he forcefully evokes his society's appreciation of human economic striving.

Competition Rules the World

There is not then only one class of Conflicts, but
there are two types on earth. One, a thoughtful man might
    praise.
The other is blameworthy. And they embody different
    attitudes.

One promotes evil war and battle, being a wretched thing.
No mortal is fond of it, but they honor grievous Conflict
    under compulsion of the deathless gods.
Dark Night bore the other Conflict, an elder child, and Zeus,
    the son of
Kronos, high-throned, dwelling in the high air, planted it
at the roots of the earth: this Conflict is much better for men.
This Conflict rouses even a quite "clueless" person toward work,
for one person has to work while looking at another,
a rich man who hurries to plow and to plant
and to put his household in order. Neighbor vies with neighbor
as he hastens after wealth. This is the good Conflict for
    mortal men.
And potter holds a grudge against potter, carpenter against
    carpenter,
and beggar is envious of beggar and singer of singer.

HESIOD, *WORKS AND DAYS* 11–26

Note here how it is taken for granted that competition and rivalry are closely associated with actual hostility. The faith that good "conflict" is beneficial toward human beings reflects a poetic grasp of the "invisible hand" of the market, where individuals' optimizing and self-centered behavior is cumulatively advantageous to all. A famous tradition among later Greeks was that Homer and Hesiod competed in poetry at a king's funeral games. Notwithstanding the prestige of Homer, Hesiod was said to have won, owing to his devotion to peaceful pursuits. However glorious war might be for the early Greeks, peace was preferable.

But why compete at all? Hesiod is also helpful about human motivation; to his mind, that goad is fear of material want and the social stigma that accompanies poverty. Here he admonishes his brother Perses, who is envisaged as a ne'er-do-well, more interested in intrigues and scams than besting his neighbor in economic advancement and improving his lot.

The Work Ethic

But, Perses of noble lineage, being always attentive to my
  instruction,
work, in order that famine hate you and fair-crowned, revered
  Demeter
cherish you and fill your barn with foodstuffs,
for famine is indeed a companion in every sense for the idle
  man.
Gods and men are angry with the man who lives idly,
being similar in his personality to the drones without stings
who waste the toil of the bees, eating in idleness. . . .
Shame that is bad accompanies a needy man,
shame that both harms and benefits men a great deal.
Shame is with poverty, but confidence is with prosperity.

—HESIOD, *WORKS AND DAYS* 298–306, 317–19

As can be seen from these passages, one great model for
large-scale organization among the Greeks and Romans was a
hive of honeybees. The elaborate cooperation of the bees,
which has only recently started to become comprehensible to
modern scientists, was marvelously mysterious to the ancients.
The ancients missed the role of the drones as impregnators of
new queens, so the drones achieved their proverbial status as
idlers, which has persisted in our own language to denote
bystanders in the game of competition.

The Greeks and Romans were well aware that successful
competition often requires deploying the essential skill, apply-
ing the right technique to a situation with the right timing.
Archilochus, the early Greek master of invective and advice,
was one of the first to use animal fables to convey such
admonishments to an audience of the seventh century B.C.

The fox knows many tricks; the hedgehog one, a great one.

—ARCHILOCHUS, FRAGMENT 201

Another ancient piece of common-sense advice about competing was to stick to your field of expertise. A homey formulation of this teaching was enshrined in Aesop's fable about the crab.

> A crab emerging from the sea was foraging on some beach. A starving fox, when he caught sight of the crab, ran up and seized him. The crab, on the verge of being gobbled up, said, "I deserve my misfortune, because, though a sea creature, I wished to become a land animal." Thus those people who leave their own customary pursuits and set their hands to matters alien to themselves usually suffer disaster.
>
> —AESOP, *FABLES* 118

A good part of successful competition involves knowing how to benefit from one's rivals in business. In *The Household Manager* of Xenophon, Socrates not only makes the obvious point that friends are assets, as much as money, but also insists that enemies can become resources for management.

> Critobulus: And according to your argument enemies are indeed assets to a person knowing how to profit from enemies. Socrates: It does surely appear so to me. Critobulus: Consequently it is the business of a good household manager also to know how to utilize enemies so as to derive profit from them too. Socrates: Most assuredly!
>
> —XENOPHON, *THE HOUSEHOLD MANAGER* 1.15

The profiting from adversaries ought not, however, to contribute to complacency, but to redoubled efforts to hone personal leadership skills, as is pointed out in one of the essaylike speeches of the fourth-century B.C. Athenian orator, Isocrates.

> But it is necessary that those able to use their minds even a little not rest their hopes of safety upon the errors of their enemies

but upon their own conduct and upon their own policies. The good result that falls by chance to our advantage through the ignorance of enemies might stop and undergo a transformation, but the advantage accruing through our own efforts should be more stable and be more long lasting for us.

—ISOCRATES, *ON THE PEACE* (8) 60

By the same token, it can be risky, even dangerous, to ignore one's rival. In some ancient treatments of his remarkable career of victory and conquest, Alexander came to be associated with injunctions of everyday practicality that were circulating in ancient society, formulated by rhetoricians for use in all sorts of mundane situations. According to his Roman chronicler, Quintus Curtius Rufus, Alexander said the following:

Go for the Knockout!

Just as for sick bodies, doctors leave nothing that might cause harm, so we should cut back everything that opposes our authority. Often small sparks having been treated with indifference have ignited a great fire. Nothing should be overlooked in a surviving enemy. Whomever you treat with contempt, you will make stronger by your negligence.

—QUINTUS CURTIUS RUFUS, *HISTORY OF ALEXANDER* 6.3.11

The temptation has always been strong, in antiquity just as today, to cope with competition by finessing it out of one's way. Just as modern businessmen have been tempted to create a cartel and carve up markets to their mutual benefit, ancient managers also tried the same collusive devices. This gambit is known from a speech of Lysias, a master of Attic prose style and oratory, whose life spanned the end of the fifth century and the first of half of the fourth century B.C. Because of various political vicissitudes, Lysias made his living by writing speeches for others. His client, the narrator in this speech, describes an attempt by grain wholesalers to collude, offering foreign grain merchants a single "take-it-or-leave-it" price per measure of their cargoes. Their ostensible reason was a public-spirited one, holding down prices for retail buyers during a time of sharply increasing prices and price volatility. Public officials had authorized the illegal purchases. Yet the wholesalers also seem to have done quite nicely out of the arrangement. When the grain merchants complained to Athenian authorities, public uproar and a trial ensued.

Doing Well by Doing Good?

Prosecutor: But perhaps they will say (as they did before the Council) that they combined to buy up grain in good will toward the city, in order that they might sell it to you as cheaply as possible. Yet I shall tell you the most important and manifest proof that they are lying. It would be necessary, if they had acted on your behalf, that they be seen to have sold grain at the same price for many days, until the stock bought in collusion was exhausted for them. But now they are selling grain with a drachma price differential [10–20 percent] in one day, as though they too [like you] were buying it by the bushel. . . . It is necessary to take to heart that it is impossible for you to vote an acquittal, because if you reject the charge when the defendants themselves admit that they colluded against the grain merchants, you yourselves will appear to be conspiring against the importers. . . . Otherwise, what do you think will be the attitude of the grain importers when they learn that you acquitted petty retailers who confessed that they had plotted against them? . . . If you condemn these men you will do the right thing and buy food more cheaply, but if not, more expensively.

—LYSIAS, *AGAINST THE GRAIN DEALERS*

(22) 5, 11–12, 17, 21, 22

Unsurprisingly, the cartel depended on official encouragement by short-sighted administrators of the grain market who
wanted to hold down prices for wheat that were spiking
upward because of international conditions. Observe also how
our speaker, rather in the mode of an ancient consumer advocate, tries to get away with the contention that punishing the
corrupt wholesalers will make grain less expensive, blithely
ignoring the many factors (like demand abroad or farming
conditions in the faraway Black Sea) affecting this largely
imported product. The outcome of the case is unknown,
although it is improbable that the grain wholesalers were actually put to death.

When the government uses its coercive power or even its
official influence to create a monopoly, we can expect those
with less political power to become victimized in the absence
of normal competition. Egypt was always one of the greatest
sources of imported wheat in the ancient Mediterranean,
because its government could extract grain in taxes from
native peasants, collecting stocks by boat. The export trade was
in the hands of Greek merchants and was always closely mon-
itored by officials to ensure that tax revenue was maximized.
When Alexander the Great wrested Egypt from the Persians
in 331, he left in control Cleomenes, a local Greek, presumably well versed in the grain trade. In an account in the treatise called the *Economics,* produced by Aristotle and his school,
we learn about what happened next.

Monopolies Can Pay!

When the local price for grain in Egypt was 10 drachmas per
bushel, Cleomenes, summoning those buying up the crop, asked
how much they wished for supplying him. They announced a
lesser price than that at which they were selling to merchants.
He said that he would pay them the price at which they were
selling to the traders. He then, setting a price of 32 drachmas,
sold the whole grain stock.

—ARISTOTLE, *ECONOMICS* 1352B

Notice both how the local middlemen give the chief politi-co their best price and how Cleomenes ingratiates himself with them by allowing them their usual price so expeditiously. The "windfall" profits for Cleomenes emerge at the next stage. The price of 10 drachmas for each measure looks a bit high for the Egyptian wholesale market. This year, however, was a time of general conflict in the midst of Alexander's invasion of Asia, so that prices may have been elevated. Nevertheless, the tripling of the final price to exporters of 32 drachmas was grossly extortionate and created a food shortage in many Greek cities.

The Art of the Deal

Negotiations were a sensitive activity in the ancient world, just as today. Everyone recognizes that both parties are seeking their own self-interest, and there is a natural suspicion that one side must come away the loser. Hence modern Americans have a strong aversion to haggling, and those hagglers par excellence, used-car dealers, have a reputation for dishonesty. We read books like that of Donald Trump to learn the chemistry needed to find "win-win" dealmaking and how "to get to yes." The Greeks and Romans had much less control over the economic process—compare our modern accounting methods—so they had to become experts at finding the terms for bringing parties together.

Our first piece of advice is that one must hold one's temper in check during negotiations. We may illustrate this truism with the delicate negotiations that took place on the eve of the massive invasion of Greece in 480 B.C. by the Persian king, Xerxes. In building their alliance, the Greek allies, led by the Spartans, approached Gelon, the strongman of Syracuse in Sicily and the major power among the western Greeks. When Gelon attempted to lay claim to the leadership of the Greek forces in return for participation, he met with an angry declaration from the Spartan ambassador that he had to accept Spartan command as a given. Herodotus, the historian of the struggle between Persians and Greeks, reports Gelon's rejoinder.

Not if We Play with My Ball!

O Spartan guest, reproaches that strike someone are likely to arouse his anger in reaction. Although you have indulged in arrogance in your speech, you have not convinced me to be unseemly in response. Since you cling so to high command, it is also fitting that I grasp it even more than you, as I am the leader of an army many times greater and of ships many more. But since your speech was put so arrogantly, we shall make some concession from our first position. If you command the infantry, I shall lead the fleet, but if it is your pleasure to lead the sea forces, I shall command the land army. And it is necessary either to be satisfied with this proposal or to depart without these allies here.

—HERODOTUS, *HISTORIES* 7.160

It is worth noting how Gelon's calmness and willingness to meet the Spartan envoy halfway with a compromise proposal puts the onus of breaking off negotiations on the Greek allies, although he does give them an ultimatum. The Athenian ambassador weighs in to protest that, although ready to defer to Spartan leadership, Athens would not be subordinated to Gelon as well. Gelon later dismissed the embassy with a proverbial observation: "Tell Greece that the spring has been subtracted from its year." That was a deft way to imply that he had the most to offer, since spring was the most pleasant season.

Another requirement for consummating a joint venture is that allies must treat each other with fairness and possess likemindedness. A good formulation of the principle is found in the opening remarks of the ambassadors of the city of Mytilene on the island of Lesbos before Spartan policy makers. The Mytileneans were trying to make a safe transition between the

Athenian league and the Spartan alliance in 427 B.C. in the midst of the intense hostilities of the Peloponnesian War.

Love Me, I'm Just Like You

Seeking your alliance, we shall speak first and foremost about justice and moral behavior, knowing that neither can friendship become solid for private individuals nor alliance for city-states in any matter, unless they behave toward each other with manifest morality and are alike in their lifestyles in general, because in divergence of judgment differences in practical matters are created.

—THUCYDIDES, *THE PELOPONNESIAN WAR* 3.10.1

The Mytilenean case is a hard one as it turns out: They have been avid collaborators in the actions of the Athenians and must now pretend otherwise to the Spartans. Their enterprise fails, and they narrowly miss mass execution for their betrayal of their former friends in Athens.

Ancient advice sometimes specified how good bargains could leave both parties happy and provide grounds for future cooperation. An instance of such thinking comes from a letter of Pliny the Younger, the imperial statesman (A.D. 61–112), whom we have met before in a number of guises. He is writing on behalf of one friend to another.

A Win/Win Situation

Tranquillus, my close associate, wishes to purchase a small property that your own friend is said to be trying to sell. I ask you to intervene so that he buys for a price that is fair, for thus he will look back on the deal with pleasure. Truly a purchase on bad terms is always disagreeable, especially for the reason that it seems to reproach the stupidity of the new owner.

—PLINY THE YOUNGER, *LETTERS* 1.24

It is interesting to realize how the deal is eased by the intervention of an important and trusted intermediary for both buyer and seller. These disinterested, but influential, parties can reassure both sides that the transaction is fair, and everyone goes away happy. So the potential for future transactions is enhanced.

6

Collegiality and Teamwork

Divide the labor; so it is lessened.

—MARTIAL, *EPIGRAMS* 4.83.8

E thics in business dealings in our modern understanding is
most certainly a topic covered in the social and political
systems of values in the ancient world. Hence, ancient authors
often exhorted people to behave justly, temperately, and brave-
ly toward each other. Instead of dealing with generalities, we
have chosen to select a few passages that directly address
norms of behavior in economic cooperation.

Because Hesiod was near the beginning of the Western tradition on work and subsistence, he often presents a classical
conception of how we ought to act toward each other in work
and business. Here is basic advice about our common attempt
to win a livelihood from the environment.

A bad neighbor is as great a misfortune as a good one is a great
advantage.
He has won a great prize who has gotten a good neighbor.

Your ox would not die unless your neighbor was bad.
Take something from your neighbor measured out fairly and
    make fair return with the same measure, and do better, if
    you are able, so that finding yourself in need later you will
    find him satisfactorily sure.
Do not profit basely: bad profits are equal to grievous losses.
Befriend someone befriending and attend one attending you.
And give to the one who gives and don't give to the one who
    does not give.
A person gives to the giving sort; no one gives to the one
    begrudging.
Give is a good girl, grab is a bad girl, herself a giver of death.
Whichever man is a willing giver, even though he may give a
    great thing,
he rejoices in his gift and feels joy in his heart.
But whoever seizes, overcome by shamelessness,
although it is some small thing, it freezes his heart.

—HESIOD, *WORKS AND DAYS* 346–363

In this passage, we see a great faith in the value of fair dealing, to the extent that a common "act of god" like the loss of
a plow ox could be averted through neighborliness. Our author
is too near the beginnings of the study of economics to understand concepts like investment, but trusts that spending on
behalf of a neighbor will bring real returns. Just as modern
communities have campaigns directed at their citizens to get
them to save and invest, archaic farmers encouraged each other
to give mutual help and so share in the eventual gains.

Contracts have to be upheld for managers to be able to
manage. The tendency to gain an advantage over partners and
competitors by chicanery can be overwhelming. In antiquity
just as today, the result was often litigation. We should all pre-
fer to believe that the side with justice on it will always pre-
vail. Yet the ancients were as skeptical as we are in our more

cynical moments. Strepsiades is one of those cranky, vulgar old farmers found in the comedy of Aristophanes. His particular problem in the *Clouds* (first produced in 423 B.C.) is that he is embroiled in many lawsuits, prompted by his delinquent debts. As we see from this passage, he visualizes the acquisition of the skills in advocacy for use in the courts as a way to win unjust victories over his adversaries.

The Wrong Approach Toward Litigation

I shall do what's necessary, trusting you, for necessity grinds me
on account of those blooded horses and my marriage, which
  wears me down.
Now I give this poor body of mine defenselessly to them
to abuse as they would, for beating, hunger, thirst,
chafing, freezing, flaying.
If I am ever going to escape my debts,
I must appear to the public
over-bold, over-endowed with tongue, brash, a mover,
a shyster, lying, a trickster,
sophistic, worn shameless in suits,
a walking law book, a castanet, a butt boy, a hole,
a supple shoe, a hypocrite, sticky, pretentious,
a felon, filthy, evasive, impossible, a licker.
If people come up to me in the street to call me these names,
let 'em do me anyway they feel like it, and, if you want,
serve me as tripe (by the goddess Demeter) for my fellow students in this institution.

—ARISTOPHANES, *CLOUDS* 439–456

The irony is that this disreputable instruction is being sought from Socrates, who for Aristophanes is an archpriest of a sect devoted to dishonest and conniving pseudo-knowledge. No matter; Strepsiades (and Socrates in his turn) will get their deserved comeuppance, as is predicted by the chorus of cloud goddesses who give their name to the play. Strepsiades' machinations entangle him in even more litigation; in retaliation for his wasted time and money, he commits arson against Socrates and his school.

The Romans also had a lot to say on fair dealing in business. In one of his satires (written around 35 B.C.), the poet Horace criticizes the "man of affairs" who is prepared to do anything for enrichment.

Lower Your Expectations

Yet a good part of mankind, deceived by false desire, says, "nothing is enough, because you're as big as your money."

What do you do with that fellow? Bid him to be wretched, since he willingly acts this way, just as that man, the one they tell stories about in Athens, filthy and rich, was accustomed to despise the gibes of the people, "people hiss at me, but I applaud myself at home, when I contemplate the coins in my strongbox."

Thirsty Tantalus grabs at streams of water in flight from his lips.

Why are you laughing? With the name changed, this story is told about you. You, sleeping and smacking your lips, are compelled to spare your money bags piled up from everywhere, as though sacred treasures, or to take pleasure in them as though fine paintings. Don't you know how far your money's good? What enjoyment it offers? Bread can be bought, vegetables, a pint of wine, and add those things without which human nature sorrows. To keep watch half-dead from fear, night and day, to fear thieves, fires, slaves, lest they rip you off and run away, does this give you joy?

—HORACE, *SATIRES* 1.1.61–78

Horace's Athenian example is none other than the misanthrope, Timon of Athens, who was the subject of Shakespeare's play. The precautions taken by some of our wealthy celebrities would fall neatly under the strictures noted by the Roman poet.

On the positive side, the ancients understood that fostering collaboration was one of the most important challenges of the successful leader. In the cooperation of neighbors in the farming community, they found one of their models for the attitude of proper team players. And from rural camaraderie could come military teamwork. Tyrtaeus was a poet active at Sparta around 600 B.C. during the Spartan struggle to retain dominance over a rich neighboring region called Messenia. Tradition states that the Spartans had sought military help from the Athenians, who sent Tyrtaeus instead of material assistance, and his encouragement of the Spartans won them victory. He provides us with an abiding image of solidarity: warriors in infantry phalanx standing shoulder to shoulder. So each protected his neighbor with his shield and the whole formation was much stronger because of its disciplined order.

Team Spirit

O young men, abiding beside each other, struggle.
And go into the close fight and among the first line fighters.
Thus fewer die and they save everyone behind.

—TYRTAEUS FRAGMENT 11.11–13

Early Greeks lived in small communities whose members had to gather for large-scale tasks, such as fortifying their towns, building temples, and manning their fleets.

Given the interests of the aristocratic audiences of epic poetry, however, most of the surviving treatments of the dangers of a failure to work together occur on the battlefield. The following sentiments from the *Iliad* of Homer nicely describe their attitude toward someone who is not a team player.

Team Playing

> Deprived of allies, outlawed, homeless is that man
> who is in love with dreadful conflict among his own people.
>
> —HOMER, *ILIAD* 9.63–64

One of the ways to promote a mindset conducive to forming cooperative ventures was envisaging human beings collaborating like the parts of a single organism. During the early Roman republic, much civil strife occurred in the evolution of the system of checks and balances within the Roman constitution. In 494 B.C. a Roman aristocrat named Menenius Agrippa quelled unrest with this famous analogy.

I Can't Believe I Ate the Whole Thing!

In the time when all the parts in a human being did not think as one, but there was deliberation and expression for each individual member, all the rest of the parts were indignantly complaining that everything through their care, labor, and service was going for the stomach, and that the stomach, quiet in their midst, did nothing other than enjoy the gratifications given it. Thus they conspired that the hands not bear food to the mouth, that the mouth not take what was given it, and that the teeth not chew what they had received. Although they wished to subjugate the stomach through famine in their anger, the individual members and the whole body came into the utmost decline. Then it became obvious that the role of the stomach indeed was not laziness, and that it was no more nourished than it nourished in returning to all the parts of the body that through which they lived and were vigorous, divided equally through the veins, perfected from digested food, namely the blood.

> —LIVY, *HISTORY OF ROME* 2.32

Marcus Aurelius, the great second-century A.D. Roman emperor, was sensitive to this traditional image. In taking respite from his political and military duties, he wrote his *Meditations,* a work based on the austere and disciplined philosophical teachings of the Greek Stoic school of philosophy. He provides an astoundingly modern conceptualization of cooperation.

Born Social Creatures

> We are born for synergy, just like the feet, just like the hands, just like the eyes, just like the rows of upper and lower teeth. So working against each other is unnatural, and being annoyed and turning one's back is counterproductive.
>
> —MARCUS AURELIUS, *MEDITATIONS* 2.1

Just as today, most leadership in the ancient world was in a thoroughly executive spirit. Therefore, sayings were coined along the lines of Lord Acton's "power tends to corrupt; absolute power corrupts absolutely." The Roman fabulist Phaedrus, who wrote in the first years of the Roman empire, sums up a story with this caution: "a partnership with men in power is never safe" (*Fables* 1.5.1). Plutarch in one of his essays (about A.D. 100) asks about the uneducated leader, "who shall rule the ruler?" (*Moral Essays* 780C). Plutarch answers his own question first by quoting the formulation of Pindar, the Greek master of choral poetry in the fifth century B.C.

> Law as the king of all, both mortals and immortals, enacting justice, controls the most violent with an irresistible hand.

Plutarch then amplifies Pindar.

> The law is not written externally in books nor on some legal notice boards, but being living reason in the soul, always keep-

ing company and being on
guard and never allowing the
soul to be deserted by its leadership.

There was also a more
democratic model for col-
laboration that became
prevalent during the fifth
century and was modeled on Athenian democracy. The
Athenians believed that the Greeks had defeated the great
Persian invasion of Greece in 480–479 B.C. because they had
been able to subordinate their national interests to the common enterprise of defense. They also argued that the best decisions were likely to come after full discussion.

Plutarch highlights this style of leadership in one of his
biographies, where he intends to recall to his contemporaries
living during the Roman Empire the traits that built their
shared culture. The Athenians were able to gather their own
allies against Persia by exemplifying a different style of teamwork from that provided by the Spartans. By their commit-
ment to the Greek cause, Cimon and Aristeides (called the
"Just"), the Athenian generals, presented a forceful contrast to
Pausanias (the Spartan commander-in-chief of the Greek
forces during 479–478), who was behaving arrogantly and
serving his own private agenda with the Persian king. A style
of collaboration fostering consensus, instead of "top-down"
command, succeeded brilliantly. The new alliance became the
basis for the international hegemony of Athens in the
Athenian "empire."

Taking Advantage of the "Ugly" Spartan

Cimon, by gently taking the side of the injured parties and
by dealing with them with generosity of spirit, imperceptibly
won the hegemony over Greece, not by force of arms, but by

discussion and character, for the majority of the allies joined Cimon and Aristeides, unable to tolerate the harshness and arrogance of Pausanias.

—PLUTARCH, *LIFE OF CIMON* 6.2

Yet the wise leader knew that some situations were so intense that a more collaborative approach might endanger an advantageous result. Thucydides considered Pericles to represent the pinnacle of leadership because of his moderation, foresight, immunity to corruption, and aversion to unnecessary risks. The following is one of the many episodes on which he based that appraisal. When the Athenians saw their territory invaded by a much stronger Spartan-led army, they were so exasperated that any discussion of the situation could risk a dangerous decision. They might leave their carefully prepared fortifications for a single huge battle that might put the survival of their empire and democracy at risk.

When Not to Call a Meeting

Pericles, seeing the Athenians both in distress regarding the present situation and not thinking in their own best interests, since he had faith that he understood best about not leaving the fortifications, did not convene a meeting of the political assembly nor any other conference, lest they on gathering in anger rather than by judgment make some disastrous mistake, and he watched over the city without turmoil as much as he was able.

—THUCYDIDES, *THE PELOPONNESIAN WAR* 2.22.1

The line between socially sanctioned cooperation that profited not only its partners but also the whole community and collusion injurious to public interest was well appreciated by the Greeks. Let us close this section with this example of sophisticated fiscal policy. Many public services are contracted out in modern municipalities through a bidding process, such as trash removal, collection of recyclables, and road repairs. In the ancient world, such private assistance of public administration could be even wider, including the collection of taxes through a process that is picturesquely called "tax farming." Athens was accustomed to contract out the collection of many of its indirect taxes on economic activity, but "tax farming" was notoriously open to abuse, as the following case illustrates. Our speaker is the early Attic master of oratory, Andocides (late fifth century B.C.), who is trying to ingratiate himself with an Athenian jury during a proceeding against himself for sacrilege. Andocides is claiming that the real animosity toward him derives partially from his service to his fellow citizens. In other words, his complaint has a familiar ring: "the special interests are out to get me." Andocides also claims to have caught a man called Agyrrhios and his syndicate colluding in the bidding for the contract to collect the import tax so as not to compete against each other. Everyone would get his share if they played along. Then Andocides realized that he could make some money while acquiring something much more valuable to him, namely credit with the Athenian jurors who might later decide his status as a pardoned criminal. Unfortunately, a presidential pardon was unavailable under the Athenian constitution.

A Sweet Deal

Now this fellow Agyrrhios, this gentleman, was the chief member of the syndicate for the collection of the 2 percent import tax for three years running. And he purchased the state contract for thirty talents. His partners were all those men who gather under the white poplar tree; what sort of persons they are, all you jurors know. They appear to me to have assembled in that location in order that twofold benefits accrue to them: that they not bid up the price in taking the contract and that all share in a contract bought for a small amount. Having made a profit of six talents and understanding how the business might be handled to yield a high profit, they formed their syndicate, and granting each other shares in the enterprise they bought the contract a second time for thirty talents.

Andocides then describes how he moved in to get a piece of the action:

> When no one was bidding against them, coming forward in the session of the Council, I kept raising counter bids until I purchased the contract for thirty-six talents. When I had sent these gentlemen packing and offered guarantors to you, I collected the money and paid it over to the city. And I suffered no loss, but my partners even took away a small profit. I stopped these men from sharing out among themselves six talents of money that was yours.

—ANDOCIDES, *ON THE MYSTERIES* (1) 133–135

7

Risk Taking

No ancient ever laid claim to the title "risk manager." Yet that term from modern business-speak is perfectly appropriate for many of those "illustrious leaders," "prudent men of affairs," and "wise advisers" we see in Greek and Roman deliberative councils. In antiquity, many people knew that a crucial feature of consulting and problem-solving is to analyze the possible outcomes of major decisions (or non-decisions). Of course, the amount of time the decision maker spent on such calculations, and what he did with them once completed, depended on his individual temperment—but also on his individual form of government. It was common in Greek states for leaders to be held personally accountable for their losses. We hear of unsuccessful Athenian generals penalized by heavy fines, exile, even death. More and more modern organizations are going that way too—that is, the insistence on executives taking personal responsibility for company losses—though of course the common remedy of a "golden parachute" to get rid of a failed CEO has far less sting than the Athenian analogues.

Now, the general attitude in antiquity toward risk and change was a little less robust than the Wall Street bulls of the late 1990s. Solon, the early-sixth-century Athenian economic reformer and canonical wise man, put it succinctly: "Count no man happy until he is dead." Grim? Sure. But life could be wildly unpredictable in the ancient Greek as well as Roman worlds, in all places at all times. Now, there were some recognized ultra-danger zones. As it happens, for ancient decision makers, perhaps the three most terrifying words were ships, battlefields, and banks.

Let's turn first to banks. Given the choice between owning a shield factory or a bank, one Athenian of the mid–fourth century calculated his level of risk and went straight for the factory:

> The income was not greater, but rather less: the factory produced 60 percent as much as the bank. Nor was the property more desirable. . . . Yet he was wise in choosing the factory. That property is risk-free, while the other enterprise involves risky revenues from other people's money.
>
> —DEMOSTHENES, *FOR PHORMIO* (36) 11

Revenue was not the only issue. Sometimes the pressure of the money-lending business became so bad that it turned into a contact sport. Or so we are told in some lines ascribed to the Roman comic playwright Plautus (late third–early second century B.C.):

> Most bankers have the habit
> of dunning every one but repaying no one,
> and if anyone duns them too insistently, they settle up with
> their fists.
>
> —PLAUTUS, *CURCULIO* ("THE WEEVIL") 377–379

Commercial sailing was in a way worse than banking. Profits might be high, but it was an all-or-nothing proposition.

A merchant has high hopes for windfalls—of which sometimes the wind holds total control.

—ANTIPHANES (FOURTH CENTURY B.C.),
FRAGMENT FROM HIS COMEDY "MELITTA" (FRAGMENT 149)

Or put more ominously,

For those who sail riskily, great profits easily make them rich—
or dead.

—MENANDER,
FROM AN UNCERTAIN COMEDY (FRAGMENT 784)

But here, one can carry caution to an extreme:

A coward when asked, "What type of ships are safer, war ships or merchant ships?" answered "Docked ships."

—PHILOGELOS ("THE LOVER OF LAUGHTER") 206

Naturally, battle, especially when it was for whole empires, was deemed the riskiest venture of all.

In private considerations there is a progression, and men rely on Fortune to varying degrees, using their discretion. But for those who desire an empire, there is no middle ground between the pinnacle of success and precipitous defeat.

—TACITUS, *HISTORIES* 2.74

Thus Tacitus, characterizing the self-made emperor Flavius Vespasianus, who used a provincial army in A.D. 69 to take over affairs in Rome, reigning for ten years until his death in the year 79, only to be followed on the throne by his sons Titus (79–81) and Domitian (81–96)—the "Flavian dynasty."

Tacitus is particularly keen to illustrate how in civil struggles there was no room for a middle way. For instance, in the warfare of A.D. 69, one general squandered an opportunity to reach northern Italy in time to face down the insurgent Vespasian's forces:

> While Fabius Valens was making his way with a large, luxurious army of concubines and eunuchs—too slowly for a combat environment—he received breaking news that the fleet at Ravenna had been betrayed. . . . He then did what is the very worst thing in a crisis. He chose a middle course, but in doing so was neither sufficiently bold nor sufficiently cautious.
>
> —TACITUS, *HISTORIES* 3.40

Obviously, if all Rome's generals were like Valens, there wouldn't have been much of an empire. Indeed, writing of contemporary events, the Jewish historian Josephus singles out the Roman military's systematic approach to risk management as one of its particular strengths. At the heart of its risk reduction strategy is taking proper counsel prior to making a decision or taking action:

> In their battles, nothing is done without advance planning, nor off the cuff, but counsel invariably precedes every action, and execution closely follows their decisions. For this reason they rarely commit errors, and even if they do, they readily correct them. They also consider grevious mistakes that follow previous deliberation to be better than chance successes owed to fortune, for this reason: because fortuitous success entices them to be rash, but consideration, even if it may sometimes end in disappointment, takes good care that the error not happen again.
>
> —JOSEPHUS, *JEWISH WAR* 3.98–100

It does not take a risk reduction specialist to identify con-cubines and eunuchs as a potential hazard for an army on the march in a civil war.

Risk Management at Work

But one wonders: Did the ancients ever develop a formal process for evaluating risk? We have seen that the designation "risk manager" will have drawn a blank with an Aristotle or a Cicero. Neither the Greeks nor Romans had an expression corresponding to "failure mode and effects analysis." And no antique "event tree" has yet been found under a rock. More's the pity, since there comes to mind Oedipus, a king of Thebes who could have used a refined instrument for assessing his exposure to risk. Here he is getting some dubious advice from his wife:

Jocasta: "What fear should mortal man have? He is ruled by
     Fortune,
    and has clear foresight of nothing.
    It is best to live at random, however one can.
    But do not fear that you will marry your mother.
    Indeed, many a man in his dreams
    has slept with his mother. But the person for whom
     these things
    hold no significance bears his life most easily."
Oedipus: "All these words you have spoken would be fine,
    if it were known that my mother was not alive. But
     now,
    since she lives, I have every reason to fear, though you
     do speak well."

—SOPHOCLES, *OEDIPUS THE KING* 977–987

One interlocutor in a Platonic dialogue does suggest that getting drunk with a prospective business partner—another recurring theme in ancient management development—is an innocent and inexpensive mode of risk assessment:

> For let's examine the options. Say a fellow has an ill-tempered and savage nature—from which spring innumerable injustices. Would you prefer to test it by entering into contracts with him at a risk to your own affairs (which is a rather perilous proposition), or by communing with him at the festival of Dionysus [among other things, god of wine]? . . . One could cite countless instances in which observing someone's character at play is clearly superior, especially since it does not involve ruinous expense. And I do not think that there are any men who would doubt that such a test of others is a respectable test, and cheaper, safer, and quicker compared to any other.
>
> —PLATO, *LAWS* 649E–650B

But that is not to say the ancients wholly lacked a developed philosophy of risk treatment. They will have understood the adage "look before you leap." Here is the story of how an individual—well, more accurately, a goat—unwisely committed himself to two separate attractive but high-risk ventures.

> A Fox fell into a deep well and found himself trapped, at a loss as how to climb back out. A Goat with an oppressive thirst arrived the same well. Putting a glad face on his misfortune, the Fox heaped much praise on the water, saying it was superb, and urged the Goat to descend. The Goat thoughtlessly leapt down. But once he quenched his thirst and was looking for the two to escape, the Fox said he had devised a stratagem that would save both of them. "I'll run up your back, and then I'll pull you up." The Goat readily humored him, now for the second time. The

Fox jumped onto his back, reached the mouth of the well, got out—and ran off.

—AESOP, FABLES 9 (ABRIDGED)

For the doctrine of informed risk acceptance, look no further than the leadership treatise of Onasander, writing in the first century A.D.:

> I am of the conviction that select soldiers should be permitted to run especially hazardous risks: if they accomplish something they are of benefit, but if they fail they do not inflict pain to the same degree. Yet to gamble away to blind luck the entire army is something I do not approve of. But I think those generals are particularly at fault who resort to the type of stratagems that in victory inflict small loss to the enemy, but in defeat significant loss to friendly forces.

—ONASANDER, THE GENERAL 32.3–4

However, some matters demanded positive risk avoidance. Plato's Socrates argued that about the high-priced consultants known as "sophists." These were teachers of rhetoric who claimed they had in stock the mode of persuasion that precisely fit the bill for whatever situation. From this bag of tricks some extrapolated further qualifications, boasting to be able to teach anyone anything, if the money was right. Here Socrates—who himself had a reputation for sophistry—insists they posed a particular hazard:

> There is in fact much greater risk in the purchase of doctrines than in the purchase of food. When you buy food and drink, it's possible to cart them off from the retailer or merchant in separate vessels. And before you drink or eat them into your body, you can lay them down in your house and seek advice,

inviting in an expert, as to what's edible, potable, or unfit to consume, and in what quantities and at what times. The result is that in this type of purchase the risk is not great. But it's not possible to cart off doctrines in a separate vessel. On the contrary, it is necessary, once you have put down the price, to take the doctrine in your very soul, and on learning it, to go off either harmed or helped.

—PLATO, *PROTAGORAS* 314A-B

Know Your Limitations

Or one can learn the first principles of risk assessment from dice players. So held the Stoic philosopher Epictetus (first–second century A.D.), himself a freed slave from Phrygia in Asia Minor (and later a star in Tom Wolfe's *A Man in Full*). He realized that it is difficult to walk the line between rash action and negligence—and to keep one's composure at the same time.

> Checkerboard-pieces are indifferent. Dice are indifferent. How do I know in what way they will fall? But once the dice have fallen, to use that cast carefully and skillfully—that is indeed my business. So also in life also the central task is this: distinguish things, stand them apart, and say, "Externals are not in my power; the ability to choose is in my power. Where shall I search after the good and the bad? Within, in what belongs to me."

But in what is foreign to you, never call anything either good
or bad, or profit or loss, or anything like that.

—EPICTETUS, *DISCOURSES* 2.5.3–5

In Plato, we find a similar suggestion, as to how folks who
are less than perfect can compensate for their flaws:

A first-rate pilot or physician distinguishes perfectly between
what is impossible in his craft and what is possible, and attempts
the one and lets the other go. Besides, if he then does make any
mistake, he is up to correcting himself.

—PLATO, *REPUBLIC* 360E–361A

Or to put that same thought in more updated form,

God grant me the courage to change the things I can change,
the serenity to accept those I cannot change, and the wisdom
to know the difference.

Balancing Risk Against Organizational Growth

Were he alive today, we can be pretty sure that the Persian
king Xerxes would not place the aforementioned "Serenity
Prayer" on the wall of his palace. Let's turn again to the story
of his preparations to invade Greece in 480 B.C. The king
was banking on the sheer size of his expedition, which was
said to number (the historian Herodotus tells us) 5,283,220
individuals plus 3,000 ships. (Never mind the modern calcu-
lation that, on the roads of those days, the head of the
infantry column would reach central Greece just when its
rear was leaving the muster point in Asia Minor.) The king's

uncle, however, pointed out that there were a few logistical snags, and offered this apopthegm:

> The best man is one who while making plans shudders in fright—reckoning all that may happen to him—but when it comes to action is bold.

> —HERODOTUS, *HISTORIES* 7.49

In this case, shuddering was in order. Mainland Greece did not have the harbors to accommodate the flotilla, and the land could not feed the Persian army as it advanced. Xerxes however downplayed the advice:

> Do not fear everything, nor think over everything to the same degree. If you wanted to calculate everything alike on every occasion that presents itself, you would never do anything. It's better, taking courage, to do everything and suffer half of what you fear than, dreading every eventuality, to never do anything. . . . How is a mere human being to know what is for certain? I think it's impossible. For the most part the rewards fall to those willing to act, rarely to those who calculate everything and hang back. You see what level of power Persia has reached. Now if those kings who preceded me had held opinions like yours, or if they had not held them but had different advisers—advisers like you—you would never have seen Persia advance to where it is now. But as it happens, facing the dangers, they did lead it forth to this level. For generally great successes are achieved by great risks.

> —HERODOTUS, *HISTORIES* 7.50

Now, in itself, the Persian king's approach to risk evaluation seems perfectly decent. But Xerxes here is meant to come off a bit as a fool—not least because he was forgetting his Persian history. Look what happened to his predecessor Cambyses

(530–522 B.C.) when he left newly conquered Egypt to invade territories further south:

> Before his army had completed one-fifth of their journey, presently all their provisions had given out on them, and after the food, the beasts of burden were eaten up until there were no more. Now had Cambyses, observing this, changed his mind and led his force back again, after his initial mistake he would have been a wise man. But paying no heed, he went ever forward. His soldiers, so long as they were able to scrape something out of the land, kept alive by eating grass. But when they came to the sandy desert, some of them performed a horrible act: they took by lot from themselves one man out of ten, and ate him. Learning of this, Cambyses grew alarmed at their cannibalising, and so gave up his expedition against the Ethiopians and marched back.
>
> —HERODOTUS, *HISTORIES* 3.25.1

There is a lesson of sorts here for the present-day CEO: Monitor developments continuously so as to identify change and minimize loss. For instance, if the world is going DVD, think long and hard about expanding your line of VCRs. If the bottom drops out of your market, the problem will not be so much the firm's staff cannibalizing each other. Rather, your competitors will be drawing lots to eat you alive.

Seize the Day

> Time is that in which there is opportunity, and opportunity is that in which there is time—but not much.
>
> —HIPPOCRATES, *PRECEPTS* 1 P. 77 K

If you know a few Latin expressions, one will probably be *carpe diem*, or "seize the day," in the poet Horace's succinct formulation (*Odes* 1.11.8). The ancients had a vivid idea on how to spot opportunity. He was a slippery customer, with an unusual haircut and no clothes. The Greek sculptor Lysippus (fourth century B.C.) had depicted "opportunity" precisely in this way, and the image won wide currency. Hence the ancient proverb "seize time by the forelock," just like an opponent in a no-holds-barred wrestling match.

> When you've found a promising thing, don't let it slip: oppor-
> tunity has hair on his forehead, but is otherwise bald.
>
> —"CATO'S SAYINGS" *(DISTICHA CATONIS)* 2.26

In other words (and there are many other versions of this), if you seize opportunity in the front, you can hold him. But once he has slipped away, he's gone forever.

For minimizing losses and identifying opportunities, Philip II of Macedon (360–336 B.C.) had few peers. Here Demosthenes compares that king's executive style to his risk-averse fellow Athenians:

> In the recent war, how in the world was that man more suc-
> cessful than we were? Athenians, I'll tell you plainly. Because he
> personally takes the field and suffers hardships and is present
> amid the dangers. He neither misses an opportunity nor neg-
> lects a season of the year. However we—for the truth shall be
> spoken—sit here idle. We are always procrastinating and passing
> resolutions and learning the latest news from the market-place."
>
> —DEMOSTHENES, *ANSWER TO PHILIP'S LETTER* (11) 17

Rewind to a point almost a century earlier, the year 432 B.C., on the eve of the Peloponnesian War. Here the Corinthians, with war against Athens practically inevitable, urge the conservative Spartans to take the initiative. But without resolve, they will be defenestrated.

Brave men . . . neither grow conceited because of their success in war nor, delighting in the tranquillity of peace, let themselves be injured. Indeed, if one hesitates for the sake of that delight, and should he remain inactive, very quickly will he be robbed of the very pleasure—namely, easy living—he seeks to maintain. On the other hand, the person who seeks further aggrandizement because of success in war has not fully considered that it is a deceptive courage by which he is elated. For if many ill-conceived plans have succeeded because they were used on still stupider opponents, there are many more, that seemed well-conceived, that ended up in disgraceful defeat. No individual executes a plan with the same confidence as when he formed it; rather, we do our conjecturing in safety, but, if we feel fear while engaged in action, we fall short.

—THUCYDIDES, *THE PELOPONNESIAN WAR* 1.120.3–5

Risk Macromanagement: Two Case Studies

Given opportunities or not, rashness was anathema to the Roman emperor Augustus (31 B.C.–A.D. 14). By chance, some of his risk policy injunctions have come down to us:

"Make haste, but slowly" [a favorite also of John Wooden, UCLA basketball coach]; "A safe commander is better than a bold one"; and "That is done quickly enough which is done well enough." Indeed, he used to say that no one ever ought to start a battle or a war, except in circumstances where the prospect of gain was shown to be greater than the fear of loss. Augustus used to remark that the type of people who chased after slight gains that involved disproportionate risk were like fishermen who used a golden hook: no catch could compensate them for its loss, if it were carried off.

—SUETONIUS, *LIFE OF AUGUSTUS* 25.4

Even in the event of loss, the stakeholders of ancient Rome were not in a strong position to hold Augustus personally accountable. Pericles as an annually elected general of Athens faced a far different situation. As we have observed, he was determined not to fight the powerful land force of the Spartans and their allies in the first year of the Peloponnesian War. So he put an unpopular risk management policy in place, and stuck to it. He had the Athenians sit tight within their city's walls—even while their property outside was being ravaged.

> He tried to calm down those who were eager to fight and were angry at the way things were going. Trees, he said, though cut and hewn, grow quickly; but once men are destroyed it is not easy to get them again. He did not bring the people together into the Assembly, fearing that it would force him to go against his judgment. But, just like the pilot of a ship, who, when a wind falls down on it at sea, arranges all things well, takes in sail, and exercises his skill, ignoring the tears and entreaties of sea-sick and frightened passengers, so Pericles locked up the city, securely garrisoned all parts of it for safety, and exercised his own judgment, caring little about those who heckled him and harbored resentment.
>
> —PLUTARCH, *LIFE OF PERICLES* 33.5–6

Pericles' friends begged him to change his policy, his enemies denounced him as a coward. Yet Pericles clung to his grand strategy, to put his trust in the Athenian fleet rather than in the land army when fighting Sparta. This decision had its political costs—including loss, for a time, of the generalship—which Pericles simply endured. Many Athenians even blamed him for the severe plague that hit Athens in 429, an epidemic that later cost Pericles his life.

The Successful Risk Manager

One advantage of developing a recognizable risk management policy is that you can use it to strategic advantage in getting the best of competitors:

A stratagem that sometimes is very effective is to pretend to be excessively on your guard and wholly averse to risk. For this often induces the enemy, letting down their guard, to make a more serious error. Or if you appear on one occasion to be bold and enterprising, it's possible by later holding back, and pretending you are about to do something, to make trouble for the enemy.

—XENOPHON, *THE CAVALRY COMMANDER* 5.15

But after racking up a winning record, don't get too comfortable in your club chair.

In social gatherings one should avoid frequent, inappropriate talk about personal exploits or perils. Though it is pleasant for you to recount your own adventures, it is not so sweet for others to listen to what's happened to you.

—EPICTETUS, *HANDBOOK* 33.14

In my opinion, for all men the future is obscure, and small occasions give rise to great events. For this reason we must be modest when the going is good, and must appear that we have an eye out for the future.

—DEMOSTHENES, *AGAINST LEPTINES* (20) 162

Finally, a parting thought from the great Roman general Scipio Aemilianus, who finally brought Carthage to its knees in 146 B.C. The Greek historian Polybius was on the spot to see the Roman commander give the order for firing the city. Here is his eyewitness account of Scipio's affect:

He turned round immediately and grasped my hand and said: "Polybius, it is a noble thing. But for some reason I have fears and premonitions, that some one else might give this order about my native land." . . . It is not easy to surpass this practical, sensible reflection. For amid one's greatest success, and the enemy's misfortune, to consider one's own affairs, possible change for the worse, and, in a word, while enjoying good fortune to keep well in mind its instability—that is the mark of a great and complete man, one worthy to be remembered.

—POLYBIUS, *HISTORIES* 38.21.1–3

8

Recognizing
Opportunity

One capital test of a first-class manager has always been the ability to recognize a business opportunity. This art usually entails seeing how to exploit resources in a new way or to meet customers' needs. In the ninth book of Homer's *Odyssey,* after serious misadventures Odysseus and his crew reach the distant land inhabited by the Cyclopes, the fierce one-eyed giants so beloved of movie special-effects geniuses. The society of these monsters is a combination of a bestial environment and a precultural paradise without the intrusion of governmental authority. The "insolent and lawless" Cyclopes live off the land, which gives them food without toil. Nonetheless, to the practiced eye of a Greek of circa 800 B.C., an island lying near Odysseus's landfall was full of possibilities. Whether the "hand-to-mouth" lifestyle of the Cyclopes is considered savage or paradisiacal, they were unable to appreciate such opportunities, and they also lacked knowledge of shipbuilding, the key technology they needed to exploit the island's wealth.

Location, Location, Location!

Now there is a wooded island that extends outside the harbor,
. . .

   Nor is the island occupied by flocks or plowed land . . . There
are no ships with painted bows for the Cyclopes, nor are there
shipbuilders among them who might labor over well-benched
ships that might fulfill each need, . . . and it is the same craftsmen who might render this island a well built community for
them. It is not bad and would produce all things in season, . . .
well-watered and fertile, and the grape vines would really never
fail. There is level plow land; they might reap a very deep crop
from season to season. . . . There is a commodious harbor where
there is no need for moorings. . . . And at the head of the harbor bright water flows, a spring beneath a cave and around it
poplars grow.

—HOMER, *ODYSSEY* 9.116–119, 123–141 (ADAPTED)

The poet envisages planting a colony on the site, where
aristocratic planners will assemble a population from Greece,
possessing various skills, who can exploit the range of
resources they have identified. That colony may even do business with the mainland opposite. Some Greek cities grew
wealthy by serving as the windows onto the world for entire
native cultures. No one would now choose to endorse the
perspective of this passage on non-Greeks, as it is clearly
formed from ethnocentric prejudice. Natives in various parts
of the Mediterranean may have appeared uncouth to Greek
visitors but they hardly qualified as real-life counterparts for
the subhuman Cyclopes. Yet Odysseus will soon explore the
possibility of developing some modus vivendi even with
Polyphemus, the Cyclops holding him captive. One can never
be too picky about overseas business connections: They can
have you for their sort of dinner, but not *as dinner*.

Identifying a market and a means to serve it need not always take on the guise of a journey with Odysseus and his shipmates over the edge of the world. It can take the form of observing a society in evolution and calmly assessing one's wherewithal to profit from the situation. An example comes from some advice offered by that paragon of perennial busybodies, Socrates. Our speaker is not, however, the Socrates of Plato with whom we are all a bit familiar; we are given a lesson from a less abstruse and chattier version of the man who is recalled by the conservative and well-traveled Athenian, Xenophon, in his *Socratic Memoirs.*

Let us listen in on Socrates' conversation with a rich Athenian called Aristarchus. Both men find themselves closed up in the city of Athens during a civil war between the present government, which is dominated by antidemocratic extremists, and the more numerous democratic forces that are based in the port of Athens and who control much of the countryside. It is the misfortune of Aristarchus that a great number of his female relations have gathered in his town house, and he is having considerable difficulties supporting them because he is cut off from the income that is generated by his rural properties. Even the ancient equivalent of a garage sale is out, we are told; there are no buyers. Socrates finds the prospect of a group of cultured people starving to death absurd and offers an alternative.

The Ancient Equivalent of a 7–Eleven Franchise?

Socrates said, "However, is it possible that Keramon ("Mr. Potter"), who is supporting so many, is not only able to supply provisions to them and himself, but also clears so much that he is even rich? . . . "Because, by Zeus," Aristarchus said, "he supports slaves, while I support free persons." And Socrates said, "Do you suppose that the free people at your house are the better people or the slaves with Keramon?" "I should think," he said, "the free folks with me." "By Zeus, he supports craftsmen, but I

support people liberally educated." Socrates responded, "Are craftsmen not persons knowing how to do something useful?"
"Certainly!" "Then," said he, "does your family know how to do
none of these [useful domestic tasks]?" "All, rather, I should
think."

—XENOPHON, *SOCRATIC MEMOIRS* 2.7.2–12 (ADAPTED)

Individuals who believe that an MBA is not always the best
training for business life will be heartened by Socrates' asser-
tion of the superiority of the liberally educated.

Nonetheless, Aristarchus objects that the other businessmen
resort to buying non-Greeks whom they train and exploit as
craft workers. Starting up a domestic "sweatshop" is not an
option for him. Socrates answers by critiquing genteel starva-
tion in idleness, asserting that by being put to work, the kins-
folk of Aristarchus will be improved emotionally, mentally,
morally, and from the standpoint of health, as well as making
money. He concludes with this statement.

Not in Front of My TV!

But as I see it now, you do not love those women nor they
you, as you are supposing that they are a punishment for you
and they see you in anxiety on their behalf. . . . If you take
charge in order that they will be at work, you will love them,
seeing them profitable to yourself, and they will cherish you
perceiving your delight in them. . . . All labor most easily, most
quickly, most well, and most pleasantly at what they understand. Do not hesitate to propose this project to them which
will profit both you and those women, and, it is likely, they
will agree with pleasure.

Aristarchus adopted this suggestion and took out a loan to
buy raw material so that his family could create a clothing
business. The portrayal of the results is reminiscent of treat-

ments of the morale and psychological strength of family firms from other times and places. This is "lifetime employment" of a particularly immediate type.

Wait Till They Get Unionized

> While working they ate lunch, after working they ate dinner, and they were happy instead of grim and instead of looking askance at themselves they saw each other with pleasure. . . . [Aristarchus] noted that they were criticizing him as the only idle eater out of all those in the house.

Socrates immediately disabuses Aristarchus of the criticism that he has no productive role. He is the manager and protector of his relatives and workers, a point Socrates underlines by comparing him in a rather homely fashion to a watchdog guarding a flock of sheep.

Naturally, not all chances for establishing profitable businesses are as dramatic as occupying a virgin territory for exploitation. Nor are all investment advisers as incisive as Xenophon's Socrates in decoding political conditions. With a stroke of intuition he realized that a crisis had suddenly made it feasible for a family business to compete against imported clothing. The devil is often in the details and it took expert and patient analysis to diagnose how to proceed.

We have just seen how Xenophon can have a Socrates transform an Aristarchus into a business "tiger," a man who previously came across a bit like an upper-class twit. Xenophon's treatise *Oeconomicus*, or *The Household Manager*, is a repository of ancient Greek thinking on managerial leadership. Here Socrates is the listener and Xenophon's mouthpiece is a rich Athenian landowner named Ischomachus. Ischomachus gives us a lesson about evaluating property for acquisition that emphasizes how the expert eye can indirectly uncover hidden value and opportunity.

Or Bribe the Lawn Service?

This is the way to evaluate another person's land regarding what it is able to bear and what it is not, by observing the crops and the trees. Whenever you understand, it will no longer be advantageous "to fight against the gods." Sowing and planting whatever the land is lacking, one will not get more output than what the earth favors in creating and fostering. If the estate is not able to reveal its own capacity because of the laziness of its owners, it is often possible from a neighboring property to know more truly about it than to find out from a neighboring man. Even land lying barren nevertheless reveals its nature, for the land producing fine wild plants is also able, when tended, to produce fine cultivated plants. Even rather inexperienced persons can just as well recognize the nature of the soil.

—XENOPHON, *THE HOUSEHOLD MANAGER* 16.3–5

Although some businesses are "sexier" than others, there is no mistaking that the successful entrepreneur must be passionate about his business specialty. It is this level of engagement with the tasks of management at hand that provokes Socrates to an ironic observation. His interjection occurs when Ischomachus reveals that he learned his expertise about the farming business from his father.

His Best Girl Was the Job

You are saying . . . that your father was a lover of agriculture . . . no less than merchants are grain lovers. Because of an intense love for grain, wherever they hear there is the most grain, merchants sail after it. . . . Then acquiring as much as they are able, they transport it through the sea . . . they do not offload it at random wherever they turn out to be, but wherever they hear that grain has the highest price and people are valuing it the highest, conveying it to these people they put it on the market.

—XENOPHON, *THE HOUSEHOLD MANAGER* 20.27–28

The grain merchant combined in his person the roles of the modern wholesaler and commodity trader, showing a love of the "futures" market worthy of a Hillary Rodham Clinton. Our passage not only portrays beautifully their optimizing business behavior, but also betrays a surprisingly modern-looking market in a fungible good. International brokers in oil products would be one contemporary analogue. They actually turn their tankers around in the middle of the ocean to head away from any place slapping price controls on crude oil and toward those willing to pay the most.

Appraisal has to be coupled with timing to make business analysis work. Calculations of value and returns are very situationally sensitive. No one from the ancient world better appreciated this point than Marcus Licinius Crassus, the first-century B.C. Roman plutocrat. He came from a family so wealthy that the epithet *Dives,* or "Rich," had become incorporated into the names of some of its members, rather as if Bill Gates were to have his name changed legally to "William Billionaire Gates." Through a combination of business savvy and political manipulations, Marcus Crassus brought his personal fortune to stratospheric regions never before reached by a Roman. One device deserves particular note. Crassus founded Rome's first fire-fighting company, staffed by specially trained slaves. A more commonplace businessman would have used his complement of men as a fire department for hire. Crassus, however, acutely saw that he had a practical monopoly on a unique capability. That made it a mechanism for adding to and subtracting from the value of property, not only his own but that of others. We may pick up with Plutarch's narrative from his biography of Crassus.

Burn, Baby, Burn!

And beside these things [buying up the property of condemned men cheaply at auction!], seeing that conflagrations and the collapses of building were disasters that were natural and endemic to Rome, because of the weight and mass of buildings, he purchased slaves who were builders and construction workers. Then, when he possessed in excess of 500 of them, he bought up burning buildings and the adjoining structures since their owners would let them go for a low price owing to fear and uncertainty. The result was that the largest part of Rome came under his control.

—PLUTARCH, *LIFE OF CRASSUS* 2.5

It is not for nothing that Plutarch was considered by our founding fathers to be their teacher on civic leadership. So he could not resist some editorializing with what he called a "blasphemous truth." Crassus "amassed his fortune out of fire and war, utilizing public calamities as his greatest stream of income." Crassus employed his wealth to gain political power. He would have heartily agreed with the maxim of Mao Zedong that "all power comes out of the barrel of a gun." Crassus used to say that no man should claim he was rich unless he could support an army from his estate!

Crassus and his band of firefighters exemplify another aspect of business leadership: Being a manager entails knowing how things are used, and evaluating assets implies insights into their utilization. Thus, reaching valuations of goods is shaped by the ways in which an individual, or for that matter a society, processes information. Socrates rigorously expands on conventional Greek thinking in another passage from *The Household Manager* of Xenophon.

In the Manager's Eye

Socrates: "These things are truly assets to the person knowing how to use each of them, but not assets for one not knowing, just as flutes are assets for someone knowing how to play the flute competently, but, for one not knowing, flutes are nothing better than useless stones."

Critobulus: "Unless he should put them up for sale." Socrates: "This now is our conclusion: flutes are assets to those selling them, but are not assets for those not selling, but still owning them, at least for those who do not know how to use them." Critobulus: "And concordantly, Socrates advances the argument for us, since it is posited that the things that profit are assets, for flutes not being sold are not assets, because they are not useful, and being sold they are assets." To these remarks, Socrates said, "If he knows how to sell, but if again he sells in return for something which he does not know how to use, not even flutes being sold are assets, in accordance with your reckoning at any rate." Critobulus: "You are likely to assert, Socrates, that not even money is an asset, unless someone knows how to use it." Socrates: "And you seem to be in agreement that assets are things from which it is possible to profit."

—XENOPHON, *THE HOUSEHOLD MANAGER* 1.10–13

It is notable how Xenophon's Socrates has a feel for the subjectivity of value and how the plans, expertise, and common sense of managers shapes the value of assets. Interestingly, he also insists that the art of selling demands knowledge. The "information age" goes back a long way, if it is really the "knowledge age" of Xenophon's Socrates.

The same entrepreneurial sense could also be applied to the assets of a whole economy. Xenophon wrote a pamphlet called *Ways and Means* that addresses ideas about restoring the financial viability of the Athenian state. One interesting exercise that he undertakes is assessing the sources of Athenian prosperity. He notes the mildness of the seasons and the length of the growing season, along with the productivity of the surrounding seas. Attica was well endowed with mineral resources, notably stone for building, but preeminently silver deposits. Athens was also well-situated geographically to act as a commercial center by land and sea, and it possessed excellent harbors. These advantages for trade were enhanced by the production of silver from the mines. Silver bullion was stamped in coins with the head of Athena on one side and an owl on the other. The Athenian "owls" were prized for their metallic purity throughout Greece, Egypt, and the Near East.

"Almighty Dollar," Meet the "Super Owl"!

Furthermore, in the vast majority of cities merchants are compelled to ship a return cargo, because they utilize money that is not usable abroad. In Athens, however, there is the greatest stock of goods that people require for exporting in exchange, but, if merchants do not wish to load a return cargo, in exporting silver they bear off an excellent trade commodity. Wherever they might sell it, everywhere they will receive a greater amount than the capital that they invested at Athens.

—XENOPHON, WAYS AND MEANS 3.1–2

Then or now, managers of private assets looked at public administration and lamented that it was not more businesslike. Most of Xenophon's pamphlet is devoted to prescriptions about improving public finances. One idea is to step up efforts to attract the international free-floating population of businessmen so that they might become resident aliens at Athens. The privileges offered would be military exemptions, the right to build homes on vacant lots, and the establishment of a special board of official protectors of their rights and persons.

Immigrant Vigor

This would make the resident aliens more public-spirited and in all likelihood the entire stateless population would desire the right of residency at Athens and they would augment the revenues of the state.

—XENOPHON, WAYS AND MEANS 2.7

This program resembles modern grants of citizenship to individuals prepared to make sizable capital investments, like émigrés from Hong Kong in British Columbia, or to persons possessing technological skills that are in short supply, such as skilled programmers in Silicon Valley. In contrast, the ancient Greeks had to battle concepts of ethnic purity before they could embrace newcomers who were ready to offer their labor and skills. Unsurprisingly, they were most ready to naturalize immigrants when they needed manpower for war.

Another set of suggestions involves the creation of a capital fund that will pay dividends to the citizens who invest in it. The investors would also receive recognition as public benefactors. This fund would be used to develop inns and hotels for visitors, facilities to conduct business, and public ships to be used as freighters. Unfortunately, we do indeed perceive the type of overselling so common in so many other public investments, such as public transit systems and sports facilities.

We Prefer Not to Call It Spending, but Investment

The majority of Athenians will get more annually than the amount they paid in the capital levy, . . . and these will be investments placed with the state, which is judged the least risky of human institutions and the most permanent.

—XENOPHON, *WAYS AND MEANS* 3.10

Xenophon's third area of advice involves the silver mines that he thinks are almost infinitely expandable, because it is practically impossible (!) to saturate the market for silver and drive down its price. The real problem is a labor shortage. Naturally, it is hard to attract new workers to mining even with special inducements. His innovation is a state-invested "rent-a-slave" business. Athens should buy non-Greek workers who can then be leased to those working the mining concessions. The business motto would presumably have been "they try harder."

Profit is the gauge against which all businesses are to be measured. In the first century B.C., Cicero gives this cynical appreciation of his fellow Romans' hardheaded attention to the bottom line.

The Profit Motive

In human affairs most men do not recognize anything as good except for that which is profitable, and they prize the most those friends, just like cattle, from whom they hope they will win the greatest profit.

—CICERO, ON FRIENDSHIP 79

The strength of the profit motive was also enshrined in a series of ancient aphorisms. The satirist Juvenal (from the first century A.D.) observes that "money lost is bewailed with unfeigned tears" (*Satire* 13, 134). Some of the most concise of these sayings derive from comedy. Roman comedy rested on Greek foundations, especially from Greek New Comedy of the late third and second centuries B.C. Here is one adage from the early-second-century B.C. Roman playwright, Plautus.

All men are experts regarding their own profits, and they show a finicky palate.

—PLAUTUS, THE TRUCULENT MAN 928

These comic meditations can take on a quite cynical aura, as a quote from the great master of Attic Old Comedy, Aristophanes, shows.

Ugh! There is no purely sound part of anyone,
   but all people are suckers for profit.

—ARISTOPHANES, WEALTH 362–363

The cost side of the profit equation also received attention. The following formulation from the *Rhetoric* of Aristotle shows that holding down expenditure as a path to profit had the force of a truism, to be found in speakers' handbooks.

> Men become richer not only by increasing their existing wealth but also by reducing their expenditure.
>
> —ARISTOTLE, *RHETORIC* 1359B

Another remark from Plautus also focuses on this aspect of the bottom line, but recognizes that there must be prior investment.

> Whoever seeks monetary gain must make expenditure.
>
> —PLAUTUS, *THE COMEDY OF ASSES* 217

The next quote expands by insisting that expenditures have to be carefully managed so that they do not overwhelm profits.

> It is not possible for profit to be created, unless there has been expenditure, I think. Nevertheless, profit will not persist, sister, if outlay exceeds it.
>
> —PLAUTUS, *POENULUS*
> ("THE LITTLE PUNIC GUY") 285–286

It was also recognized in the same tradition that there could be advantageous expenditure on people as well.

> On a bad wife and an enemy, if you spend anything, it really is expenditure. But on a good host and friend, what is expended, is profit.
>
> —PLAUTUS, *THE BOASTFUL SOLDIER* 673–674

There are always, however, individuals, lacking focus on the purposes of management, who preferred to think about the results of succeeding rather than about the means to succeed. One such fantasy is described by the fifth-century B.C. Greek lyric poet Bacchylides.

The Daydreamer

Wine sends soaring aloft the anxieties of men:
right then one is destroying the fortifications of cities,
he expects to become monarch over all mankind,
his houses gleam with gold and ivory, and
his freighters carrying wheat bear the greatest riches from Egypt.
In this way the heart of the drinker is stirred.

—BACCHYLIDES FRAGMENT 20B.10–16

9

Communication

Although the ancient world was devoid of telephones, beepers, fax machines, or voice mail, it depended absolutely on effective oral and written communication. In fact, much of what we practice today in terms of speechmaking, public debate, business writing, and decisionmaking can be traced directly to the Greeks, who intensely respected and intensively exploited the power of logos—word or reason. The democratic institutions of the ancient Athenians—assembly, council, law courts—depended on the ability of citizens to formulate and grasp oral arguments. Rhetoric, the art of speaking, truly flowered in later-fifth-century Greece, although its practitioners were often criticized for making the worse argument appear the better—and although the first teachers of rhetoric, known as the sophists, inadvertently bequeathed us a pejorative for clever but misleading argument: "sophistry."

The Whole Truth?

Our earliest work of European literature, Homer's *Iliad,* raises the single toughest issue in communications: whether to tell the truth, especially when that truth happens to be inconvenient or downright detrimental. One may be tempted to prevaricate. Frequent prevarication, however, destroys a person's credibility. Now, as it happens, the swift-footed hero Achilles was a stickler for honesty, and this is how he prepared to tell a visiting delegation what he really thought:

> It is necessary to proclaim my word without shilly-shallying
> how I think and as it will be accomplished,
> that now one and another of you not wear me out with
> your presence.
> That man is as hateful to me as the gates of Hades,
> who hides one thing in his heart but says another.
>
> —HOMER, *ILIAD* 9.308–313

Still, complete candor may not work so well in the boardroom. For a more pragmatic approach, try the hero Odysseus, "the man of many ways," as he was known, who endured much—and invented stories freely whenever he needed to get out of a scrape. His words were not to be trusted, yet the glancing-eyed goddess Athena admired him and in the *Odyssey* offered him this backhanded praise:

> A shrewd and wily man it would be
> who could get past you with all your tricks, even if a god
> contended with you!
> You wretch, you schemer, never tired of tricks—you wouldn't
> even in your own land
> give up deceits and thieving stories, which are part of you
> from head to foot.
> But come, let's not speak of this any longer; we both know
> plenty of tricks, since you are the best of all mortals in
> counsel and stories, and I am known among all the gods
> for craft and cunning.
>
> —HOMER, *ODYSSEY* 13.291–299

Maintain a Dialogue

Either way, whether you tell the truth or not, you should keep the lines of communication open, since negotiation is generally preferable to armed conflict. Herodotus tells how a royal adviser to the Persian king carefully explained the usual Greek method of warfare, which consisted of pitched battle between massed ranks of heavily armed men who hailed from rival city-states. The adviser then commented on what seemed to him the sheer absurdity of Greek fighting Greek:

> Yet since they speak the same language and share the use of heralds and messengers, they should settle their differences in any way but fighting.
>
> —HERODOTUS, *HISTORIES* 7.9C

Left to themselves, Athenian citizens did a lot of talking in open-air assemblies on the Pnyx, a low hill in view of the Acropolis. Once they acquired their fifth-century empire, which gave them brief dominance over numerous city-states dotting the Aegean coasts and Greek islands, they sometimes faced painful dilemmas that called for protracted debate. Perhaps their most famous dilemma concerned the citizens of Mytilene, principal city on the island of Lesbos, which in 428 B.C. revolted from Athens and had to be punished. As the historian Thucydides tells it, the Athenians met in assembly and voted harsh measures: the men of Mytilene were to be executed, the women and children sold into slavery. The next day, however, the Athenians had second thoughts, best expressed by a man named Diodotus, who urged the importance of talking things through:

> I neither blame those who have reopened the Mytilenaean issue—nor praise those who object to repeated deliberation on the weightiest matters. But I do believe there are two things

most opposed to good decisions: haste and passion. The former goes along with folly and the latter with an ignorant and deficient judgment. As for speeches—whoever contends that they should not guide our affairs is either stupid or is pursuing some private interest of his own.

—THUCYDIDES, *THE PELOPONNESIAN WAR*
3.42.1–2

Presentation Counts

To act effectively in the ancient world, one had to speak well. In fact, the art of speaking lay at the heart of all transactions, business or otherwise. We know a lot about it, not least because the fourth-century Greek philosopher Aristotle devoted a treatise to the subject. He taught that the key to excellence in rhetoric rested on three components: logos, logical argument; pathos, the emotion the speaker stirred in his listeners; and ethos, the persona or character the speaker managed to project. He identified, in turn, three qualities that contribute to effective ethos:

There are three things that give a speaker credibility. . . . These are good sense, virtue, and good will. . . . Therefore the man who seems to have all these qualities will necessarily be believed by those who hear him.

—ARISTOTLE, *RHETORIC* 1378A

In other words, people won't listen to you if they think you're unreasonable, corrupt, or malicious. A passage from the *Iliad* further suggests that one should cultivate good grooming and avoid picking fights, lest one's oratorical skills go to waste. Through the figure of Thersites, an uncouth and contemptible character, Homer shows how not to speak in public. Thersites is ugly, shrill, absurd—and the hero Odysseus threatens to send him packing if he doesn't keep his mouth shut.

> Whatever [Thersites] thought seemed ridiculous to the Greeks,
> and he was the most ill-favored man who came to Troy;
> he was bandy-legged and lame in one foot, his shoulders
> were concave, drawn together over his chest, and above
> he was point-headed, and a sparse fluff of hair was on top.
> . . . Then once again he raised a shrill cry against
> godlike Agamemnon and uttered accusations. . . .
> But godlike Odysseus was quickly beside him,
> and he looking askance at him, upbraided him with a harsh rejoinder.
> "Thersites, reckless speaker, however clear-voiced an orator you may be,
> check yourself and do not be willing to quarrel with kings. . . .
> If I chance on you again raving as you are just now,
> . . . I shall send you crying to the swift ships,
> whipped from the assembly with shameful blows.
>
> —HOMER, *ILIAD* 2.211–264

Pliny the Younger, in the early second century A.D., also commented on effective speaking. He had studied rhetoric with the famed Quintilian and then went on to pursue a highly successful career as a Roman lawyer and magistrate. Here he notes the role of pacing and momentum—and the importance of knowing when to stop:

> The very success of my speech persuaded me to fall silent and stop, for it is rash not to rest content when things are going well. Moreover, I was afraid that the strength of my body would fail with a renewed effort, for it is more difficult to start again than to go straight on. There was also the danger that the rest of my speech would seem cold, as if laid aside, or tedious if resumed. Just as torches guard their flame if continually brandished but renew a lost spark only with great difficulty, so too the warmth of the

speaker and the attention of the audience are maintained by continuity but grow weak when interrupted or diminished.

—PLINY THE YOUNGER, *LETTERS* 4.9.10–11

Despite the centrality of rhetoric, the ancients were well aware that actions speak louder than words. Yet Demosthenes, the famous fourth-century B.C. Greek orator, had to make this point again and again to his fellow Athenians, some of whom were unwilling to face the fact that Philip II of Macedon, considered by many a quasi-barbarian from the north, was poised to take over the independent city-states of classical Greece. To combat Philip's assurances that his intentions were good, Demosthenes delivered a series of speeches against him called, quite appropriately, the Philippics. Cicero, the famed Roman statesman of the late Republic, used the same title in his diatribes against Marc Antony hundreds of years later, hence our word *philippic,* denoting any caustic verbal attack. Here is an excerpt from the Third Philippic in which Demosthenes entreats his fellow citizens to get the message:

If the other party [namely Philip II], wielding weapons and considerable personal power, bandies talk of peace but in fact uses his resources for war, what else remains but to defend ourselves?

—DEMOSTHENES, *THIRD PHILIPPIC* (9) 8

Don't Waste Words

The Spartans, who lived in Laconia, were famous among the Greeks for their brevity of speech—hence our word *laconic.* In Spartan society, which was devoted to the perpetuation of a disciplined warrior elite, starting from the age of seven boys were trained in endurance, aggression, and self-sacrifice. They also learned that words should be as sharp as weapons:

They taught the boys to use speech that mingled sharpness with grace and compressed much thought into a few words. . . . For as the semen of men who have sex too often becomes infertile . . . so too does incontinence in talking make one's speech empty and mindless. Therefore, when a certain man from Attica jeered at the Spartan swords for being so short . . . , King Agis said, "And yet certainly we reach our enemies with our daggers." And I see that although the speech of the Spartans seems short, it certainly reaches the heart of the matter and grabs the listener's attention.

—PLUTARCH, *LIFE OF LYCURGUS* 19.1–2

Even today, a few well-chosen words make for the best sound bites, whereas a plethora of verbiage merely obfuscates a speaker's meaning. Herodotus tells an amusing story about Spartan brevity of speech. In the sixth century B.C., exiles from the Greek island of Samos, it seems, came to Sparta and asked for an expeditionary force that would take back their homeland from the tyrant Polycrates and restore them to power:

Coming before the authorities, they said a great many things about how much they needed help. The Spartans at this point answered that they had forgotten the first words spoken and did not understand the last. After that, coming before them a second time, the Samians said nothing at all but this: carrying a sack, they said, "The sack needs grain." The Spartans answered, "You wasted the word 'sack.'" But they decided to help them.

—HERODOTUS, *HISTORIES* 3.46

In fact, the Spartans did mount an expedition: They laid siege to Samos for forty days, but the unyielding Polycrates either exhausted their patience or bribed them with counterfeit money, whereupon they gave up and went home again.

Keep Some Messages Confidential

The "Eyes Only" envelope has been largely superseded, perhaps, by confidential e-mail messages accessible only to a recipient with the correct log-on and password, or even by encrypted cell phone conversations that keep unwanted third parties off the line. Yet there are ways to defeat any security system, and privacy remains an issue for anyone who wants to exchange useful gossip or hatch a master plan that will surprise and overwhelm the competition. In antiquity, there were all sorts of reasons to send secret messages—while fomenting rebellion, for example, or revising strategy—and there were all sorts of ways to do it. One could, for example, sew up the message inside dead game, as did a disaffected Mede named Harpagus when he wanted to help place Cyrus on the throne of Persia:

> Since the roads were guarded, he had no other way to convey a message so he contrived the following: He cleverly prepared a hare, both slitting its belly and taking away none of the fur, and just as it was he put inside a paper on which he had written his plan. Once the hare's belly was stitched up, he gave it to the most trusted of his servants along with hunting nets, and sent him to the Persians. He instructed the man to give Cyrus the hare and to tell him by word of mouth to cut open the hare with his own hands and to make sure no one else was present when he did so.
>
> —HERODOTUS, *HISTORIES* 1.123

This method was a bit messier than today's certified mail, but it worked. And Histiaeus, a despot of the city of Miletus in southwest Turkey, had an even brighter idea that helped him instigate a revolt of the Ionian Greeks again the overlordship of Persia. To his confederate he sent a cleverly tattooed messenger:

For Histiaeus, wishing to signal Aristagoras to revolt, had no safe way of doing so because the roads were guarded, so he shaved the head of his most trusted slave, tattooed a message on it, and waited until the hair grew back. As soon as it did, he sent the slave off to Miletus with no message other than this: when he came to Miletus he must tell Aristagoras to shave his hair and look at his head.

—HERODOTUS, *HISTORIES* 5.35

Don't Let Messages Go Astray

This trick succeeded, but at a later date Histiaeus let down his guard, with the result that several important messages were treacherously misdelivered to the Persian governer Artaphrenes, against whom Histiaeus was plotting. The results were fatal.

After that, Histiaeus . . . sent letters to some Persians in Sardis. But [the messenger] did not give the letters to the people to whom he had been sent, but took and put them in the hands of Artaphrenes. And Artaphrenes, when he had learned all that was going on, ordered [the messenger] to take the letters and deliver them as Histiaeus had originally instructed. . . . Artaphrenes then killed many of the Persians.

—HERODOTUS, *HISTORIES* 6.4

In modern terms, beware of carelessly directing a private e-mail message to a routine list of recipients that may include enemies as well as friends. In a hostile environment, make sure your message reaches the intended party without being intercepted. Julius Caesar once had a close call while trying to send a message into an allied camp that lay under siege. How was he to slip a piece of paper past the enemy guard? Well, he ordered a soldier to hurl inside the fortifications a spear to which the letter was attached. Caesar later wrote:

> By chance it stuck in a tower, nor was it noticed by our troops for two days. On the third day it was observed by a soldier, taken down, and duly delivered.
>
> —JULIUS CAESAR, *THE GALLIC WARS* 5.48

Listen Promptly and Make Prompt Replies

Pliny the Younger often praised the emperor Trajan and he extolled his boss's skill at communicating with representatives of farflung cities and provinces who sought an audience with him at Rome. As usual, Trajan is represented as the master of managerial aplomb, whom many a CEO would do well to emulate when dealing with branch offices at home and abroad:

> We see how he answers the petitions of the provinces and even the prayers of separate cities. He makes no difficulty over granting audience and no delay in responding. People get in to see him immediately, they are dismissed promptly, and at long last there is no excluded crowd of delegates besieging the doors of the emperor.
>
> —PLINY THE YOUNGER, *PANEGYRIC ORATION* 79.6

A good executive secretary can make sure there is no excluded crowd of employees and business contacts besieging the doors of the powerful executive; efficiency and openness, as Pliny shows, should be explicit goals.

Use Express Delivery

Without e-mail, air mail, or even old-fashioned delivery trucks, it could be tough getting messages from Point A to

Point B, but the Greeks employed long-distance runners to act as couriers. For us, the most famous of these is the man who in 490 B.C. is said to have run from the battlefield of Marathon to the city of Athens with news of the Greek victory over Persian invaders. That distance, as everyone knows, was about 26 miles; the name of the runner varies in our written sources, which are actually late and rather insecure. A less known but even more impressive runner was a man named Phidippides, also associated with Marathon, but he did his running before, not after, the battle. According to Herodotus, he ran from Athens to Sparta, a distance of about 150 miles, to ask the Spartans to fight against the Persians. This would be like running from New York to Albany, or from Florence to Rome. What's even more remarkable is that he reportedly reached his destination as swiftly as Federal Express.

First, while still inside the city, the generals sent to Sparta a herald named Phidippides, an Athenian man who was a long-distance runner and highly trained . . . and reached Sparta the day after he had left Athens.

—HERODOTUS, *HISTORIES* 6.105–106

The Persians, on the other hand, invented a kind of Pony Express, and in ancient Gaul the Celts combined fire beacons and loud shouts to send messages from one hilltop to the next; they reportedly needed only four days to relay information in this fashion from one end of France to the other. The Romans were the most famous of all for their system of communication. To start with, they were expert builders of roads, bridges, and viaducts: records made during the reign of the emperor Diocletian in the late third century A.D. reflect a total of 372 roads covering a distance of about 53,000 miles. The use of this road system was first perfected by the emperor Augustus:

So that what was going on in each province could be announced and understood more swiftly and promptly, [Augustus] at first posted young men at moderate intervals along the military roads, and thereafter, carriages. The latter proved more convenient, since the same men who carry through letters from a given place could also be questioned, if events demand it.

—SUETONIUS, *LIFE OF AUGUSTUS* 49.3

10

Management-Employee Relations

A s every modern businessperson knows, one should strive to maintain healthy relations between employees and management. This was doubtless true in ancient Greece and Rome as well, and managers faced a host of issues that are still alive today: how to encourage hard work and high performance; how to instill loyalty; how to promote; how to cultivate teamwork and collaboration; how to exert authority without going too far. On the other side of the coin, anyone below the rank of tyrant or emperor had to decide how to treat his boss. Prosperity and success in almost every enterprise, in fact, depended on a finely calibrated and harmonious hierarchy of interpersonal relations.

Understand Your Work Force

Aristotle offers several shrewd observations on the subject of human resources. In his day, most of the urban workforce in Greece consisted of slaves who were owned as private property; some of Aristotle's management concepts, however, can be readily applied to modern-day wage slaves. The great fourth-century B.C. analytical philosopher draws useful distinctions between middle managers and common laborers. He also suggests how to get the most out of both:

> Of possessions, the foremost and most necessary type is the best and most economic: the human being. It is necessary first of all to put in place energetic slaves. There are two types of slaves, the managerial and the laborer. Since we see that training makes the young what they are, it is indispensable for those slaves to be entrusted with that category of tasks suited to free men that they be readied aptly. . . . It is necessary that a goal also be fixed for all slaves, since it is fair and advantageous that the prize of freedom be available. They are willing to work when there may be a prize and a period defined. It is also necessary to take hostages by slave procreation.

> —ARISTOTLE, *ECONOMICS* 1344A–B

Even in an ancient society that practiced slavery, the manager nonetheless needed strategies that would enable him to identify talented individuals, groom some of them for positions of responsibility, and set goals that would bring out the best in everyone. Although the structure and status of the workforce has, thankfully, changed, certain fundamental issues have not.

Don't Throw Out the Dress Code

In our society, attire reflects rank and also reinforces it. We expect workers to look like workers and bosses to look like bosses. In Aristotle's day, however, the Athenian dress code for slaves, whether of the managerial or laboring sort, apparently did not differ much from the dress code for ordinary citizens and other free men. It was business casual for both, which probably meant a loose-fitting tunic and flat sandals. The lack of status markers such as wingtips, silk scarves, or a

$200 haircut, however, had a leveling effect that some citizens resented, as this passage from the late fifth century B.C. shows:

> There is the greatest wantonness of slaves and resident aliens at Athens and it is not permitted to strike with your stick there, nor will a slave stand aside for you. I shall tell the rationale for this local practice: if there were a law that the slave, resident alien, or freedman might be struck by a free person, one would often lash out, thinking an Athenian citizen was a slave. The common people are no better dressed there than slaves and aliens, and they are no better looking.
>
> —"THE OLD OLIGARCH,"
> *THE CONSTITUTION OF THE ATHENIANS* 1.10

Keep Them Working

Aristotle recommended employing only those people who were deemed energetic. A high value was placed on the ability to work. In fact, the so-called Protestant work ethic that still governs us today is not without antecedents in the ancient world. In a largely agricultural economy there was no place for idleness—unless, of course, one was already rich. Hesiod, a Greek poet circa 700 B.C., admonishes his brother to embrace work and eschew idleness:

> Gods and men are angry with the man who lives idly,
> Let it be dear to you to set in order tasks that will be well arranged,
> So that your barns be loaded with seasonal production.
> Out of labors men become rich in sheep and wealth,
> and engaged in labors they are much dearer to the immortal gods.
> Work is no cause for blame, but idleness is blameworthy.
> And if you work, soon an idle person will envy you as you grow rich, for virtue and glory wait on wealth.
>
> —HESIOD, *WORKS AND DAYS* 303, 306–313

Win Their Loyalty

Loyalty in an employee is well worth cultivating, a point that seems to have been lost lately amid buyouts, mergers, and dot-com companies. Gone is the staid and heartwarming job security offered by earlier corporate giants, like Bell Telephone in its monopolistic heyday. Gone, too, is the sense that one should act in the best interest of one's employer—or employee. But what would the ancients say? Would they think this was any way to run an enterprise or weather a storm? We doubt it. In fact, first-century B.C. Roman statesman and orator Cicero suggests that, in a crisis,

> There is need for both loyalty and speed.
>
> —CICERO, *LETTERS TO HIS FRIENDS* 11.26

Genuine loyalty, according to the fourth-century B.C. Greek historian Xenophon, will shine forth in adversity:

> For to show loyalty amid prosperity is nothing special, but when men show themselves true friends in adversity, this is remembered for all time.
>
> —XENOPHON, *HISTORY OF GREEK AFFAIRS* 4.8.4

A passage in Herodotus implies that the loyal cooperation of subordinates can be secured by generous pay and benefits that will allow them to indulge in personal luxuries, spend time with the family, and pursue harmless hobbies like . . . well, lyre-playing. The time is 546 B.C., the place is western Turkey, and the Persian invader Cyrus the Great has just conquered the Lydians, whose captive monarch actually tells Cyrus how to keep the populace from rebelling:

> Showing pardon to the Lydians, lay on them the following command, so that they will neither revolt nor be threatening

to you. Sending word to them, forbid them to possess weapons of war and order them to wear soft tunics beneath their cloaks, and to lace theatrical booties on their feet, and tell them to teach their sons to strum the lyre and pluck the strings and go into small trade. And swiftly, king, you will see them turned into women instead of men.

—HERODOTUS, *HISTORIES* 1.155

Misogyny aside, the point here is that Cyrus knew how to preempt dissidence and generate loyalty. And his methods worked well for him. He went on to found the great Persian empire, which centered on modern Iran but soon encompassed lands from Pakistan to Egypt and the Balkans.

Don't Be Subtle

Julius Caesar, intent on maintaining a position of power in republican Rome during the 50s B.C., made sure that his subordinates knew exactly to whom they owed their gratitude:

To gain security for later times, [Caesar] always made a great point of placing the year's magistrates under obligation to him. Nor did he help any candidates—or allow them to be elected—except those who agreed to champion him when he was out of town. And he did not hesitate to exact an oath from some, or even a written contract.

—SUETONIUS, *LIFE OF JULIUS CAESAR* 23.2

Handle Promotions with Care

In the ancient world, as in today's world, rank had its privileges. Certain Greek and Roman writers, moreover, insist on the importance of maintaining a clear hierarchy. Not everyone in an organization is created equal, they suggest, nor should everyone be treated in the same way. In a letter to a friend and colleague, Pliny the Younger writes in the early second century A.D.:

> But I can't refrain from giving you praise that sounds like advice—praise for the way you maintain class distinctions and protect rank. If these are tossed together in disorder and confusion, nothing is more unequal than the so-called "equality" that follows.
>
> —PLINY THE YOUNGER, *LETTERS* 9.5.3

One should hand out promotions in a systematic fashion, according to logical Xenophon, always raising the rank of the most effective officers and always making sure that they enjoy the promotion.

> All these officers were entitled to be waited on by their subordinates, and other honors appropriate to each then followed.
>
> —XENOPHON, *EDUCATION OF CYRUS* 2.1.23

On the other hand, subordinates who arrogate power to themselves should feel the lash:

> For in a well-managed household no one comes forward and says to himself, "I should be the manager." And if he does, the master, after catching him insolently giving orders, drags him out and flogs him.
>
> —EPICTETUS, *DISCOURSES* 3.22.3

We, however, recommend a tongue-lashing as more appropriate in this litigious age. Much can be accomplished with a proper dressing-down or a well-timed demotion. But promotions, above all, must be handled with care because

Nothing is more troublesome than a low man when he rises to
a high position.

—CLAUDIAN, *AGAINST EUTROPIUS* 1.18

If a low man is troublesome, an overrated horse is bound to
be even more so. The emperor Caligula created considerable
resentment when he conferred favors and luxuries upon his
favorite equine, named Incitatus.

In order that the horse Incitatus might not be disturbed,
[Caligula] used to send soldiers around the day before the games
to impose silence in the neighborhood. Furthermore, he gave him
a marble stall, an ivory manger, purple blankets, and a collar of
jewels. He even gave him a house and servants and furniture, so
that guests invited in his name might be received more splendid-
ly. It is also said that he had resolved to make the horse a consul.

—SUETONIUS, *LIFE OF CALIGULA* 55.3

Incitatus would be in good company with modern cats and
dogs who have inherited stock portfolios.

Teach Them to Get Along—Up to a Point

Cyrus the Great, who built the Persian empire through guile
and conquest, was greatly admired for his ability to manage
men—so much so that almost 200 years later, the Greek
writer Xenophon wrote a historical novel, the *Cyropaedia,*
using the life and exploits of Cyrus as a framework for his own
ideas on leadership. Cyrus, we are told, thought that subordinates should be treated with great even-handedness and,
moreover, that they should get to know each other:

A military company consisted of 100 men. They lived in tents
according to their companies, for Cyrus thought that tenting

together would benefit them in the coming conflict: they saw each other provided for in the same way, and there could be no pretext of disadvantage that could allow anyone to prove less brave than another in the face of the enemy. And Cyrus thought that if they tented together, they would also benefit by getting to know one another . . . since a feeling of respect was more likely to be engendered in them all, while those who don't know one another seem somehow more indifferent, like people in the dark.

—XENOPHON, *EDUCATION OF CYRUS* 2.1.25

This bit of advice speaks well for the company picnic. But the process of getting to know each other can be carried too far, as the Roman emperor Trajan explains to Pliny the Younger in the early second century A.D. Pliny is the imperial governor of Bithynia-Pontus, along the Black Sea coast of modern Turkey. He has just suggested, in the wake of a devastating fire in the capital, Nicomedia, that a fire company be formed there. But the wise and dour Trajan, in a letter to Pliny, says no, because he fears the firemen may form a union of sorts:

It may well have occurred to you that one could form a company of firemen at Nicomedia like those found in many cities. But we bear in mind that your problematic province and mainly its cities have been stirred up by associations of this sort. Whatever name we give them and for whatever reason, those who come together for a common purpose soon turn into a political club.

—PLINY THE YOUNGER, *LETTERS* 10.34

Be Accessibile

We are often reminded that keeping the lines of communication open is the best way to solve problems and forestall trouble. Cicero, writing in the first century B.C., gives almost modern business advice when he insists that the executive's door should always stand open:

> Let access to you be extremely easy. Open your ears to the complaints of all. Don't let the needs or wants of anyone be shut out from this popular access and the tribunal or even from your home and bedroom.
>
> —CICERO, *LETTERS TO HIS BROTHER QUINTUS* 1.1.25

Americans have traditionally observed a stricter distinction between home and office than the Romans did. Nevertheless, beepers and cell phones do follow the busy executive into his or her bedroom, like it or not. Keep in mind that the emperor Trajan, very early in the second century A.D., won high praise for making himself wonderfully accessible to his magistrates, at the same time creating an atmosphere that can be best described as casual. Pliny writes:

> And you yourself, how you receive everyone, how you wait! How you spend a large part of your days on so many cares of state, yet maintain an atmosphere of leisure. So we, no longer pale and terrified, no longer slow in approaching as if in danger for our lives, but now secure and cheerful, we come to you when it suits us. Even if the emperor has sent for us, sometimes there is something urgent that keeps us at home; but we are always excused by you, and never do we have to make excuses. To be sure, you know how eager we all are to see you and call on you,

and you all the more freely and generously hold out opportunities for this pleasure.

—PLINY THE YOUNGER,
PANEGYRIC ORATION 48.1–2

There is, on the other hand, such a thing as being too accessible. This was the lesson Julius Caesar learned on the Ides of March in the year 44 B.C. He entered the senate house that day in an open and casual manner but quickly found himself surrounded:

> As he sat down, the conspirators took their places around him on the pretext of business, and immediately Tillius Cimber, who had assumed the leading role, came nearer as if he were going to ask something. When Caesar declined and, with a gesture, put him off to another time, Cimber grabbed his toga at both shoulders; then, as Caesar cried, "But this is violence!" one of the Cascas stabbed him in the back, just below the collar-bone. Caesar seized Casca's arm and jabbed it with his stylus, and tried to jump up but was checked by another wound. When he saw that he was hedged on every side by drawn daggers, he wrapped his head in his toga and at the same time, with his left hand, drew its folds down to his ankles so that he might die with greater dignity, with the lower part of his body also covered. And thus he was stabbed with twenty-three blows, uttering only a wordless groan at the first blow—even though some have reported that to Marcus Brutus, as he attacked, Caesar said, "You, too, my child?"
>
> —SUETONIUS, *LIFE OF JULIUS CAESAR* 82.1–2

The dignity with which Caesar accepted death is notable, but his twenty-three wounds suggest that despite the casual atmosphere in the senate house that day, he had misread the situation.

Don't Lose Your Cool

A casual atmosphere can also encourage bad behavior, if those who ought to know better let their guard down. A story told of Alexander the Great suggests that the chief executive officer should at all times hold his temper and resist provocation. This is what happened. Alexander and a favored subordinate were deep into a drinking party when the subordinate, whose name was Cleitus, insinuated that Alexander was a lesser man than his late father Philip II:

> But [Alexander] jumped up and, as some say, snatched a spear from one of the guards and with it struck Cleitus and killed him. . . . I pity Alexander for this misfortune because at that point he showed himself defeated by two vices by which no self-controlled man should be overcome: passion and drunkenness.
>
> —ARRIAN, *ANABASIS* 4.8.8–4.9.1

Do the Best You Can with Difficult Superiors

The story of Alexander and Cleitus raises another issue: If distinctions of rank are to be maintained, what can subordinates do when their boss exhibits crazy or dangerous tendencies? The Roman emperor Nero, who ruled in the first century A.D., is still known for his debauchery, sadism, and insane selfishness. Few people realize that for the first five years of his reign, the Stoic philosopher and playwright Seneca tried to shape the young man into a passable human being and viable ruler. Among other things, this distinguished subordinate tried to improve his boss Nero with treatises on mercy. These offer a grim irony, as Seneca vindicates fairness, goodness, piety, integrity, honesty, and moderation—and praises Nero for his kindness:

Now certainly it is fitting that men should conspire for fairness and goodness as soon as envy, from which arises every evil of the soul, is expelled. It is fitting that piety and integrity, along with honesty and moderation, should rise again, and that vice, having abused its long reign, should at length give place to an age of happiness and purity. It pleases us, Caesar, to hope and trust that for the most part this will happen. The kindness of your heart will be delivered, will be diffused little by little throughout the entire body of the empire, and all things will be formed in your likeness.

—SENECA, *ON MERCY* 2.1.4–2.2.1

Though Seneca's influence, while he served as adviser to the young ruler, seems to have worked for a while, making possible perhaps five years of good governance, Nero was not destined to inspire the masses with his "kindness of heart." Seneca, as his influence with Nero gradually declined, decided to bow out. He turned over most of his wealth to the emperor and retired to philosophize and write. Eventually accused of participating in a failed plot to assassinate Nero, he was forced to commit suicide.

Flattery Will Get You Somewhere

Fortunately, not every boss is criminally insane, and successful dealings with most of them can be enhanced by deft and well-timed flattery. In the ancient world, in fact, shameless sucking up was the key to getting on the boss's good side. A Persian courtier named Mardonius, for example, pays his king Xerxes an ageless compliment:

Master, you are not only the best of all the Persians who have ever been, but of all that shall ever be.

—HERODOTUS, *HISTORIES* 7.9

If delivering a speech like that is too embarrassing, one should at least remember the boss's birthday. It isn't necessary to send flowers or a cigar; a well-chosen card will do. The wording that Pliny the Younger came up with to honor the emperor Trajan's birthday is well worth imitating:

> I pray, sir, that you find this birthday and many more to come as happy as possible, and that safe and sound, and with eternal praise, you may increase the flowering glory of your reputation with new deeds laid upon the old.
>
> —PLINY THE YOUNGER, *LETTERS* 10.88

Pliny admits elsewhere that he would rather praise than advise, since praise is always welcome and risk-free:

> To tell the emperor how he should behave is a worthy but burdensome and almost arrogant task. Certainly, to praise an excellent emperor and in this way to shine a beacon light that posterity may follow, offers much utility and no presumption.
>
> —PLINY THE YOUNGER, *LETTERS* 3.18.3

At the risk of contradicting himself, Pliny also remarks that one should avoid looking like a flatterer:

> Once I had been named consul I abstained from anything that looked like flattery even if it really wasn't, not so much because I was independent and secure in my position, but because I understood our emperor. I saw that the highest praise I could offer him was this: that I utter nothing as if compelled to do so.
>
> —PLINY THE YOUNGER, *LETTERS* 6.27.2

If Pliny is right, there is an art to flattery—a way to do it without being detected. Aeschylus, the great Greek tragedian of fifth-century B.C. Athens, warns that some bosses know obsequious behavior when they see it:

> But whoever is a good and discerning shepherd cannot be taken in by men's eyes, which seem to reflect a gladness of mind but only fawn with watered-down affection.

—AESCHYLUS, *AGAMEMNON* 795–798

11

Motivation

How do you make people burn to excel? How do you elicit their finest ideas, their greatest energy, their utmost effort, and an all-round positive attitude? In other words, how do you make them deliver? These are venerable questions, as old as human laziness, and it is fascinating to find that writers in ancient Greece and Rome articulated strategies that we still see in today's organizations. Now, as then, the canny executive must think very hard about how to keep his or her employees maximizing production. The best way to do it, of course, is by offering incentives. The basic concept of incentives, both positive and negative, has changed little since classical antiquity: If you want people to work hard, give them a reason.

Offer Them Cash

That reason can vary according to the situation, but cash incentives usually work well. Love of money may be the root of all evil but it is also one of the most persistent facts of the human condition. The sixth-century B.C. Greek poet Theognis, for example, says most people think wealth is more important than anything else:

For the greater part of mankind this is the one achievement.
"Get rich!" . . .
There is no advantage to anything but wealth,
Not even if you know how to make counterfeits look genuine,
or possess the eloquence of godlike Nestor,
or can run faster than the Harpies
and the swift children of the North Wind, whose feet are
    instantly swift.
No, everyone should store up this adage:
That wealth everywhere has the greatest power.

—THEOGNIS 1.699–718

Aristophanes, the most famous comic playwright of fifth-century B.C. Athens, argues that if people already had all the money they wanted, they wouldn't do another lick of work:

If Wealth were to see again and distribute himself equally,
No one of mankind would practice either a craft or field of
    knowledge.
Once these two endeavors had been abolished for you, who
    would wish
to be a bronze-smith, or build ships, or sew, or make wheels,
or cut leather, or make bricks, or launder, or be a tanner,
or break the earth with plows to harvest the crop of Demeter,
if it would be possible for you to live in idleness without both-
    ering about all these things?

—ARISTOPHANES, WEALTH 510–516

Actually, history has proven Aristophanes wrong, since the rich generally work quite hard to get even richer. Then again, he was referring only to physical, backbreaking hard labor of the sort that major players in leveraged buyouts and venture capital need never do. But let's get back to the subject of cash incentives. Cyrus the Great, as Xenophon tells us in his treatise on that ruler's education, was canny about handing out cash:

> And when he came back to Media, he gave his captains as much of the money as each deemed sufficient, so that they in turn would be able to reward any of their own men whom they admired; for [Cyrus] thought that if each one made his division praiseworthy, the whole army would do well for him.
>
> —XENOPHON, *CYROPAEDIA* 3.3.6

This worked a lot like a year-end bonus. Love of money also ensured the efficacy of outright bribes, however, which might occasionally be used to achieve noble goals. A splendid example of this is found in the pages of the historian Herodotus, who tells how the Athenian statesman and admiral Themistocles was induced to make his stand against the Persians off the Greek island of Euboea in 480 B.C.:

> But when [the Euboeans] failed to persuade [the Spartan Eurybiades], they went to Themistocles, the Athenian commander, and gave him a bribe of thirty talents, for which the Greek forces were to stay there and fight to defend Euboea.
>
> —HERODOTUS, *HISTORIES* 8.4

Now, a talent was a lot of money. It was worth 6,000 drachmas, and we know that later in the century, a drachma per day was excellent pay for a skilled worker. So Themistocles accepted this tidy sum. He then had to figure out how to get the other Greek captains to keep their ships in position at the strategic anchorage of Artemesium, since there was no clear chain of command that ensured their adherence to his plan.

The thing to do, as he quickly surmised, was to pass along a little of the money he had received:

> And Themistocles did the following to keep the Greeks there: to Eurybiades he gave five talents of this money, pretending that he gave it from his own means. When Eurybiades had been persuaded in this way [the Corinthian], Adimantus . . . alone of all the rest said he would sail away from Artemisium and not stay; to him Themistocles said, swearing, "No, you at least will not desert us, for I will give you a greater gift than the king of the Medes would send if you deserted your allies." He said this and at the same time sent to Adimantus' ship three talents of silver. So these two men were won over by gifts, and the Euboeans were obliged, and Themistocles himself profited; he kept the rest of the money without anyone knowing.
>
> —HERODOTUS, *HISTORIES* 8.5

Offer Them Honors and Prizes

Bribes were an important kind of incentive but by no means the only one. Xenophon urges the use of prizes and public dinners to spur both officials and entrepreneurs to do their jobs well, rather like the annual awards ceremony embraced by so many organizations. Never underestimate the appeal of a free meal. Xenophon also says that officials should be encouraged to resolve disputes with dispatch so that commerce at harbor or market can proceed briskly. To that end, he says, offer them more prizes:

> If someone would legislate prizes to the officials of the commercial harbor and market for whoever settled disputes most fairly and expeditiously, so that a litigant wishing to depart would not be prevented from doing so, in this way a much greater number would conduct commerce more advantageously.
>
> —XENOPHON, *WAYS AND MEANS* 3.3

Xenophon wants entrepreneurs to keep bringing in business and believes that the honor more so than the gastronomic pleasures of state-sponsored dinners would act as an incentive:

> It would also be good policy and a good advertisement to honor merchants and ship owners and to have occasions for public hospitality when there might be invited those who are seen to benefit the city with the most important ships and cargoes. Persons honored in these ways would be eager not only for the sake of profit but also of honor to visit us as though coming to their personal friends.
>
> —XENOPHON, *WAYS AND MEANS* 3.4

Keep Them Guessing

Money, prizes, and free meals are all positive incentives, but the ancients also knew a thing or two about negative incentives. There were any number of nasty punishments too unpleasant to catalog here, and without clear parallels in the corporate world, but a character in Xenophon's fictional *Education of Cyrus* usefully points out that fear can be even more persuasive than pain:

> "And so do you think," Tigranes said, "that men are enslaved by anything more than by terror? Don't you know that those who are beaten with the sword, which is considered the strongest punishment, are nevertheless willing to fight again with the same enemy? But when people are really terrified of someone, they cannot look him in face even when he's appeasing them."
>
> "You mean," said Cyrus, "that terror punishes men more than actual harm?"
>
> —XENOPHON, *EDUCATION OF CYRUS* 3.1.23

The emperor Caligula, who ruled Rome from A.D. 37–41, definitely ruled by fear rather than by love. In some cases, he

used discomfort and humiliation to keep high-ranking senators from challenging his authority. The image of toga-clad
Roman senators running alongside Caligula's conveyance or
waiting on him hand and foot at his banquet couch is irre-
sistible, although the next level of abuse is more sinister:

> He was no more respectful or kindly toward the Senate, letting
> some who had held the highest magistracies run in their togas
> beside his chariot for several miles; when he dined, he let them
> stand beside his couch or at his feet, girded with a napkin.
> Others, once he had secretly put them to death, he continued
> to summon as if they were alive, and after a few days he would
> lie and say they had committed suicide.
>
> —SUETONIUS, *LIFE OF CALIGULA* 26.2

Caligula found lengthy and protracted forms of capital punishment the most effective:

> "He hardly ever let anyone be executed except by numerous
> small blows, in accordance with his constant and soon well-
> known command: 'Strike so he may feel he's dying.' . . . Often
> he repeated the tragic verse: 'Let them hate me, so long as they
> fear me.'"
>
> SUETONIUS, *LIFE OF CALIGULA* 30.1

Be Like Alexander the Great

If Caligula resembles a psychotic
mob lord, Alexander the Great may
exemplify the model CEO, particularly in his use of incentives. Along
the way to conquering most of the
known world, this charismatic
leader encountered many formidable
obstacles. There were the great distances
to be traversed, the inclement weather, the

unwieldly baggage train, the occasional battle. He marched from Greece through Turkey to the Syro-Palestinian coast, from there to Egypt and back again, thence through Mesopotamia onto Persia and beyond. Deep in Afghanistan he decided to take an apparently impregnable fortress perched high on a rock. Alexander offered prizes to the first men to the scale the rock:

> Then Alexander announced that there would be a prize of 12 talents for the first man to go up, and for the second man, a second prize, and for the third, so on and so forth, until the last prize for the last man to go up would be 300 [Persian] darics. And this announcement spurred on the already eager Macedonians.
>
> —ARRIAN, *ANABASIS* 4.18.7

On many other occasions he was observed to reward and praise those who worked hard and punish those who shirked:

> Alexander himself stood by as an observer; he praised anyone who was trying hard, but punished anyone who was forsaking the task at hand.
>
> —ARRIAN, *ANABASIS* 4.29.7

When the situation became so dire that the men could no longer be controlled by rewards and punishments, Alexander wisely turned a blind eye. Once, his army was so hungry that pack animals were being slaughtered for food. On this occasion, he did not try to stop them:

> And the things that were happening had not escaped the notice of Alexander, but he saw that the remedy for present circumstances was his pretence of ignorance rather than his knowing acquiescence.
>
> —ARRIAN, *ANABASIS* 6.25.2

Make Them Better People

It is appropriate to give Pliny the Younger, a dignified and effective Roman imperial magistrate, the last word on rewards for virtue and vice. He was convinced that proper incentives properly applied could improve a person's character:

> Men of similar sort are spurred on by this reward for honesty and industry, while dissimilar men are enticed, since rewards for virtues and vices make men good or bad. Few people are so strong in character as to do the right thing, or shun the wrong, whether or not it turns out well for them. And when the reward for labor is given to idleness, the reward for vigilance to torpor, and the reward for frugality to extravagance, other men start to pursue the same things they see some obtaining undeservedly. They wish to seem and be like those men—and as they wish, so they become.
>
> —PLINY THE YOUNGER, *PANEGYRIC ORATION* 44.7–8

Provide a Good Work Environment

Life in the modern business environment is full of stresses and strains that stem, in part, from technological advances that ever quicken the pace of transactions and force more items onto a single day's agenda: briefings, interviews, conference calls, consultations, staff meetings, strategy sessions, business trips, plant tours, power lunches. Yet the ancient world, even without beepers and cell phones, could be busy enough. As Pliny the Younger once complained in a letter to a friend:

> New business matters get added to the old before the old are finished, and the column of tasks, like so many links in a chain, stretches out further every day.
>
> —PLINY THE YOUNGER, *LETTERS* 2.8.2

Even the most sympathetic CEO will never be able to eliminate all sources of stress, but he or she can do a lot to create a working environment in which managers and employees alike are encouraged to let off steam from time to time.

Take Time Off in the Country

Pliny's friend Caninius Rufus owned a lovely colonnaded house on Lake Como. His house, as Pliny observes, had baths full of sunshine, admirable dining rooms, and a fine view of lake and stream (Pliny the Younger, *Letters* 1.3.1). Up there in the north Italian countryside, in the foothills of the Swiss Alps, a well-to-do Roman had several ways to relax:

> Are you reading or fishing or hunting or doing all three at once? For all things can be done at once at our Lake Como. The lake has fish, the woods that ring the lake have game, and that deep retreat of yours offers ample chance to study. Whether you do all those things or only one thing, I can't say I begrudge it. I am just bothered that I can't do the same, though I long for these diversions as sick men long for wine, baths, springs.
>
> —PLINY THE YOUNGER, *LETTERS* 2.8.1–2

Grab a Towel and Head to the Baths

Fishing and hunting were popular pastimes, equivalent to modern golf, raquetball, or workouts at the fitness center. But baths and bathing throughout classical antiquity were a favorite way to let off steam, or, in a more literal sense, to revel in it.

> Baths, wine, and sex corrupt our bodies—but they make life.
>
> —*CORPUS OF LATIN INSCRIPTIONS (CIL)* 6.15258

The Romans had an intricate system of bathing, with tepid, cold, and hot pools housed in opulent buildings sometimes the size of Grand Central Station. In fact, our great nine-teenth-century train terminals were modeled on immense bathing establishments like the Baths of Caracalla, built on thirty acres in Rome between A.D. 206 and 217. These baths were walled with fine imported marbles of varied hues, floored with intricate mosaics, and roofed with soaring arches that enhanced the mood of citizens who came to soak in lux-ury. The Roman poet Statius rapturously expresses the idea behind bathing:

> Begone, oh toil and care, while we sing of baths that glitter with gleaming stones. . . . Come, young goddesses, turn your pure faces this way and bind up your shining hair with tender gar-lands while wearing not a stitch! Thus you emerge from deep springs and torment your satyr-lovers with the sight.
>
> —STATIUS, *SILVAE* 1.5.9–18

The Greeks, in their heyday, seem to have cared more for exercising in gymnasiums than reclining in baths. They proved their manly vigor and athletic skill by hurling the discus, for example, or running foot races. Yet one character in the com-edy *Clouds* of Aristophanes, produced in 423 B.C., objects to a new and fashionable trend that was luring young Athenians away from the rigors of training. The name of this conserva-tive character is Right Logic, who faces off against Wrong Logic. Their rhetorical sparring, incidentally, is likened to a wrestling match.

> Wrong Logic, *aside:* Watch how I put to shame the education he relies on. . . . *Turning to his opponent:* First of all, they say you don't approve of bathing in warm water. On what grounds do you condemn hot baths?

Right Logic: On the grounds that they're the pits—and make a man a coward.

Wrong Logic: Hold on! For now I've got you around the middle and you'll never get away. Tell me—among the sons of Zeus, which man was best?

Right Logic: I, for my part, judge no man better than Herakles.

Wrong Logic: Well, where did you ever see Baths of Herakles with cold water? Yet who was ever braver than he?

Right Logic, aside: It's arguments like this that fill the baths with jabbering youths and leave the gymnasiums empty!

—ARISTOPHANES, *CLOUDS* 1043–1054

In any case, the Greeks clearly understood the joys of relaxation as well as today's tired executives understand saunas and jacuzzis. The historian and ethnographer Herodotus tells us, moreover, that even the Scythians, a wild and nomadic tribe of horsemen who inhabited the north shore of the Black Sea, knew how to relieve stress:

Whenever the Scythians get the seed of this hemp, they creep under felt mats and then throw the hemp on stones that are red-hot with fire; and, having been thrown, it smolders and releases so much steam that no Greek vapor-bath could surpass it. The Scythians howl in their delight at the vapor-bath.

—HERODOTUS, *HISTORIES* 4.75

More power to them! Frankly, it was tough being a barbarian. The Scythians were under constant social pressure to kill the enemy and drink from his gilded skull. They also had to collect scalps. If a man had neither scalp nor skull to show at the end of the year, he was not permitted to drink from the great bowl of wine that the king specially prepared. Then again, if the king died, there was more pressure, more trouble. Herodotus says the Royal Scythians, during the funeral rites,

sliced off bits of their ears, shaved their heads, cut their fore-
arms, tore their foreheads and noses, and drove arrows through
their left hands (Herodotus, *Histories* 4.71). Then came the
burial itself, which involved an awful lot of digging and some
stressful human sacrifice:

> And in the rest of the space inside the barrow they bury one of
> his concubines—having strangled her—and also his wine-bearer
> and his cook and his groom and his man-servant and his mes-
> sage-bearer and his horses and the first-fruits of all else and his
> golden drinking cups.
>
> —HERODOTUS, *HISTORIES* 4.71

Who wouldn't want to spend time in the sauna after dealing with a major restructuring?

Have Another Drink

A couple of microbrewed beers at the nearest theme bar seem
pale by comparison, but Greeks and Romans alike were big
on the ritualized drinking party, which in Greek was called a
symposium. Although the modern event by that name is stuffy
and boring, the word itself is derived from the Greek for
"drink" and "together." Aristocratic males used to imbibe at a
symposium while reclining on couches; when conversation
grew dull, they enjoyed their dancing girls, flute-players, and
the like; the idea was to avoid talking shop:

> I don't care for the man who, while drinking wine beside the full
> mixing bowl,
> Speaks of quarrels and tearful war,
> But rather one who, by mingling the bright gifts of Aphrodite
> and the Muses,
> Recalls the good cheer of the feast.
>
> —ANACREON, *ELEGY* 2

Know When to Give Up

Some problems seem easier to face after a hot tub or a dry martini; a little relaxation can go a long way toward the discovery of creative solutions. Some problems, on the other hand, are insoluble. If so, the best course is to bow to the inevitable and give up. Indeed, that may be the only way to lower stress and keep one's blood pressure on an even keel. The little-known Marcus Bibulus, for example, was probably not interested in succumbing to a heart attack. This unfortunate man had to deal with serving as consular colleague of the glorious Julius Caesar in 59 B.C. He became totally frustrated because Caesar was determined to run Rome all by himself—and could get away with it because, among other things, he enjoyed considerable name recognition. After a time, Bibulus acknowledged defeat and after that stopped going to the office:

> [Caesar's conduct] drove him to such desperation that, until his term ended, he stayed locked up in his house and did nothing but announce adverse omens via proclamation.
>
> —SUETONIUS, *LIFE OF JULIUS CAESAR* 20.1

This flexible work arrangement can also be viewed as a precursor of telecommuting. But it had its downside. Although our Bibulus was merely being realistic, the act of giving up exposed him to a certain level of ridicule:

> After that, Caesar managed all the affairs of state alone and as he wished; so that some witty fellows jokingly pretended to sign official documents with the words: "Done in the consulship of Julius and Caesar" instead of "Done in the consulship of Bibulus and Caesar."
>
> —SUETONIUS, *LIFE OF JULIUS CAESAR* 20.2

Don't Let Things Get to You

Undoubtedly the CEO faces the highest levels of stress when things aren't going well, when events simply do not turn out as planned. This happened to Emperor Augustus in A.D. 9 when three of his Roman legions, under the leadership of Quintilius Varus, were ambushed and slaughtered in the untamed Teutoberg Forest in Germany.

> In fact, they say [Augustus] was so upset that for months on end he let his beard and hair go uncut, and sometimes he dashed his head against a door, crying "Quintilius Varus, give me back my legions!"
>
> —SUETONIUS, *LIFE OF AUGUSTUS* 23.2

But bashing one's head against the wall is not the best way to cope with stress. The better course is simply to lighten up. An especially clear lesson in stress management can be drawn from the exotic world of the ancient Near East, where a king named Amasis dominated the Egyptians. He firmly believed that everyone must relax sometimes, so he did all his business in the morning and spent the rest of the day carousing with his friends in what amounted to a long Happy Hour. As Herodotus recounts, the king's friends finally asked him why he didn't sit haughtily on a throne all day long so that his subjects would be duly impressed. And Amasis replied,

> Men who possess bows bend them only when they need to use them. If bows were bent all the time, they would break, and therefore would be of no use when needed. This is also the nature of a man: if he wanted to work hard all the time and never allowed himself time to play, he would go mad without knowing it, or have a stroke. Knowing this well, I give each activity its turn.
>
> —HERODOTUS, *HISTORIES* 2.173

12

Hiring and Firing

We have all seen the large stacks of résumés that come flooding in, via e-mail or snail mail, whenever any attractive job opening is advertised. Naturally, it is gratifying to know that so many people want to take advantage of "a great opportunity in a growing global company," for example, and that so many are willing to "assume multiple responsibilities" in an "empowered team environment" so as to build "cutting-edge careers" that will "shape [their] future and the industry itself." Still, from an employer's standoint, picking the right person for the job, especially from a large pool of applicants, is by no means easy. How can one see into the hearts and minds of prospective employees and select the one who truly fits the bill? Conversely, how can one get rid of a bad hire in a timely fashion and avoid incurring a lawsuit?

Scrutinize Their Résumés

In the early days of the Roman emperor Trajan's reign (A.D. 98–117), Pliny the Younger gave the new emperor some sage advice. He said Trajan should look at their prior job experience and hire only those men who had worked for his worthiest predecessors such as his adoptive father Nerva or, we may imagine, the good Vespasian and his son Titus. In other words, henchmen of the late Domitian and aging flunkies of the long-dead Nero need not apply:

> First of all, employ no one unless he was evaluated and selected either for you or your father or one of the best emperors. Then, train these men daily so that they measure themselves against their own rank, not yours, and become all the more worthy of our esteem because it is earned and not taken for granted.
>
> —PLINY THE YOUNGER, *PANEGYRIC ORATION* 88.3

Pliny had advice not only for employers but for employees as well. He emphasized that job candidates, rather than sit around waiting for a phone call from the imperial office, should build their résumés by working hard to distinguish themselves:

> It's best if office is sought through office, and honor through honor.
>
> —PLINY THE YOUNGER, *PANEGYRIC ORATION* 70.8

Check Their References

The next step after screening out applicants with unsavory pasts is to check their references, another age-old practice. We are fortunate to possess actual letters of recommendation written by Cicero in the first century B.C. and by Pliny the Younger early in the second century A.D. The letters anticipate and answer the sorts of questions that a prospective employer thought important. Here is a sample letter by Pliny the Younger, written to support the application of an aspiring young lawyer:

> The man you want is Voconius Romanus. His father was renowned in the order of knights . . . and his mother comes

from a leading family. He himself recently held a priesthood in Nearer Spain. . . . When we were students together, I firmly and dearly admired him. . . . No one could be a more faithful friend or more agreeable companion. He is wonderfully charming in conversation, face, and expression. Added to this, he has an intellect that is naturally excellent and has been trained, through handling lawsuits, to be discriminating, pleasant, and supple. . . . Now that you know the sort of man he is and how much I esteem and love him, I ask that you provide for him in accordance with your own rank and disposition.

—PLINY THE YOUNGER, *LETTERS* 2.13.3–10

Notice the emphasis on family background, which still works for the Bushes. Then observe the deliberate mention of how Pliny came to know the job candidate and the glowing praise for the man's talents and overall demeanor. Does it sound familiar? Does Pliny's friend sound too good to be true? Still, might as well bring him in for an interview. Such letters must often have had the desired effect, since Pliny kept cranking them out. At one point he wrote the following to the prefect of Egypt on behalf of another friend:

Maturus Arrianus is the leading citizen of Altinum, and when I say "leading" I am not speaking of his riches, which are extremely plentiful, but of his purity, justice, dignity, and wisdom. I follow his advice in business and his judgment in research, for he is a man of great honesty, great candor, and great intelligence. He loves me as much as you do, and I can say nothing warmer than that.

—PLINY THE YOUNGER, *LETTERS* 3.2.1–4

Did Pliny say, "I am not speaking of his riches"? And yet he spoke of them! One may particularly admire this rhetorical strategy in which a speaker or writer mentions a vital point, while pretending to deny its importance. To be fair, though, many of Pliny's letters of recommendation were perfectly straightforward. Here is one addressed to the emperor Trajan to support the application of a man who apparently was Pliny's subordinate rather than his friend:

> I have found your freedman and procurator Maximus, sir, throughout the time we have been associated, to be upright, industrious, and conscientous. He is as attentive to your affairs as he is firm on discipline. I gladly supply this attestation with the good faith that I owe you.
>
> —PLINY THE YOUNGER, *LETTERS* 10.85

Pliny very appropriately focuses on the work habits and moral capacities of the job candidate. The statesman Cicero, on the other hand, writes one rather nauseating letter that highlights the applicant's propensity for slavish gratitude and ass-kissing:

> Hagesaretus Larisaeus, promoted by my great favors during my consulship, was mindful of his debt, and grateful too, and subsequently devoted himself to me with great diligence. I highly recommend him to you as my friend and intimate acquaintance, as a person who knows the meaning of gratitude, as a good man and a leading member of his community who is most deserving of your friendship. You will make me very grateful if you let him know that this recommendation has carried great weight with you.
>
> —CICERO, *LETTERS TO HIS FRIENDS* 13.25

Consider Their Personal Habits

If Roman letters of recommendation place as much emphasis on character as on competence, a passage from the fourth-century B.C. writer Xenophon shows that a similar point of view obtained in the Greek world. Here Xenophon explains how to select a housekeeper:

> We established a housekeeper by considering who seemed to us most self-controlled with reference to eating, drinking wine, sleep, and intimate relationships with men, and in addition to these criteria, who seemed to have the best memory and foresight in order that she not get a bad mark from us through carelessness and that she should figure out how she might receive some token of regard from us by gratifying us in some manner.
>
> —XENOPHON, *THE HOUSEHOLD MANAGER* 9.11–13

It isn't easy to find an employee who is at once abstemious, clever, careful, and eager to please. Add to that a bit of wisdom, once again from Pliny the Younger, who observes that a person who needs less sleep can get more done. In this excerpt, Pliny is trying to explain the prolific brilliance of his uncle, Pliny the Elder. He cites the quality of the late man's intellect, and also the fact that he had at his disposal so many waking hours in a day:

> Do you marvel that such a busy man [Pliny the Elder] completed so many volumes, many of them so demanding? You will marvel still more when you learn that up to a certain age he practiced law, that he died in his fifty-sixth year, and that in between his time was full and hindered by important offices and his friendship with the emperors. But he had a sharp intelligence, an amazing zeal, and the greatest capacity to do with little sleep.
>
> —PLINY THE YOUNGER, *LETTERS* 3.5.8

Make a Decent Offer

Once the résumés have been sifted, and the references checked, once the leading candidates have passed your subtle questioning, there arrives the crucial moment when you find out whether your top choice will actually take the job. At this point, a great deal hinges on diplomacy. There's a right way to make an offer, and more than one wrong way. Interestingly, our earliest version of a job offer in the Western world is found in Homer's *Odyssey*, which tells of the home-coming of the hero Odysseus to his native Ithaca, where in his long absence 108 rude suitors have beset his lovely wife Penelope. In this passage a suitor named Eurymachus is offering—or pretending to offer—a job to a beggar who is actually Odysseus in disguise. Note that Eurymachus provides several details about the purported job but remains vague on pay and benefits.

> He spoke, and at once he addressed Odysseus the sacker of cities.
> "Stranger, would you like to work for me, if I should take you on,
> in an outer farm—your pay will be adequate—
> whether gathering building stones or planting great trees?
> There I would provide you annual substinence,
> dress you with clothes, and put shoes on your feet."
>
> —HOMER, *ODYSSEY* 18.356–361

What on earth is "adequate" pay? Where is the medical package? And why doesn't Eurymachus mention a retirement plan? Then, for some reason, he delivers a purely gratuitous insult:

> Yet since you have learnt bad occupations, you would not wish
> to undertake work, but wish to beg among the people
> in order that you are able to feed your gluttonous stomach.
>
> —HOMER, *ODYSSEY* 18.362–364

This sort of remark is both unnecessary and unwise, especially if the person at whom it is aimed happens to be a great warrior and sacker of cities. Needless to say, when Odysseus later sheds the disguise and fights to take back his royal house, Eurymachus is one of the first to die, shot in the chest by the hero's unerring arrow.

Bring Them on Board

Now, as soon as an offer has been made and accepted, it is important to make the new employee feel like part of the corporate family. Whatever slot the person occupies on the organizational chart, he or she needs to embrace the interests of the company. This passage from Xenophon continues the exemplum of the housekeeper:

> We taught her to be sympathetic to us by giving her a share of our joys when we were happy and, if some sorrow occurred, by inviting her to share this. And we educated her to be eager to increase our household by making her have an understanding of it and giving her a share of its success.
>
> —XENOPHON, *THE HOUSEHOLD MANAGER* 9.11–13

So basically they offered her profit-sharing. This was not a bad idea, even back then.

Create More Jobs If You Can

Plutarch, in his *Life of Solon,* explains how the great Athenian lawmaker tried to relieve underemployment in the early sixth century B.C. at a time when both the city of Athens and the surrounding region of Attica were being flooded by immigrants. There was not enough farmland to go around, so Solon wisely encouraged growth and job creation in the craft industries, which would have included pottery manufacture, metalworking, and the like:

Observing that the town was being filled up with people continuously flowing into Attica from every direction for security, that the greater part of the territory was infertile and useless, that traders were not in the practice of importing to people with nothing to give in return, Solon directed the citizens toward the craft industries, and he passed a law that it was not required for a son to support his aged father if he did not teach him a trade. . . . But Solon harmonized the laws to circumstances and not circumstances to laws, and, observing that the nature of the land was barely suitable for farming, not being able to support an idle and underemployed mob, he accorded great status to the crafts, and he mandated that the Council of the Areopagus [that is the Athenian "Senate"] examine from which occupation each citizen took his means of subsistence and punish the idle.

—PLUTARCH, *LIFE OF SOLON* 22.1.24

Never Fire a Key Person

There is a season to hire and a season to fire. Nonetheless, one should keep in mind that virtually every business operation has at least one individual on board who is truly indispensable. As the 6th century B.C. Greek poet Theognis—and any downsizing expert—will tell you, that person is not the one to can:

"...They have deposed the ship's pilot, that good man who was
    standing guard with expertise.
They seize possessions by force, and order has been destroyed.

There is no longer an equitable division, in the common interest,
   but the passengers, merchandise carriers, rule, and the base are
   on top of the noble.
One could be aware of future misfortune, if one is wise.

—THEOGNIS 682

Don't Be Overly Hasty

If you must fire key players, don't be overly hasty. A negative example of how not to fire is found in Herodotus, who tells how the Persian king Xerxes reacted to the failure of his first bridge across the Hellespont in 480 B.C. An act of God had taken out the bridge, but Xerxes blamed both the sea and the hapless engineers:

As soon as the strait had been bridged, a great storm fell upon it and cut the cables and broke them up. He commanded that the sea should be punished [by lashing, branding, and cursing— as we shall later see], and that the men who had supervised the bridging of the Hellespont should have their heads cut off.

—HERODOTUS, *HISTORIES* 7.35

We are left to imagine how the next set of engineers felt about their task of building a replacement bridge. It's safe to say, however, that arbitrary punishments seldom boost morale.

Don't Send Mixed Messages

Another story about Xerxes depicts a manager who had not thought things through. The Persian monarch was having trouble coping with the recent debacle at the Battle of Salamis, in which the puny city-states of Greece overwhelmingly defeated his mighty empire. Bitterly humiliated, and wondering how he would explain this to his mother, Xerxes was retreating by sea from Greece to Turkey when high winds threatened his ship. It apparently was carrying too many people, and the helmsman told Xerxes that it would sink unless some of the royal courtiers on deck could be gotten rid of:

> And it is told that when Xerxes heard this he said, "Men of Persia, now let each of you show how much he cares for his king. For in you, it seems, lies my safety." That is what he said, and the men first prostrated themselves before him and then leapt into the sea, and the ship, having been made lighter in this way, came safely to Asia.

So far, so good. But wait until you see how Xerxes treated the helmsman, who had shown himself to be loyal, shrewd, and competent:

> As soon as Xerxes got out onto land, he did the following: because the helmsman had saved the life of the king, he bestowed upon him a golden crown; but because he had lost so many Persians, he cut off his head.
>
> —HERODOTUS, *HISTORIES* 8.118

Handle the Matter Discreetly

Still, we all know there is a time and a place for getting rid of a person who is neither indispensable nor blameless nor even particularly competent. One ancient precedent suggests that after you've decided whom you're going to fire, you should deliver the news behind closed doors and with no extra people in the room:

> The Spartans, when they execute people, do so by night and never by day.
>
> —HERODOTUS, *HISTORIES* 4.146

13

Delegation

Stripped to its core, management is about getting other folks to do jobs for you. And to get things done through others, you have to delegate authority. Here Greek literature provides some memorable instances in the "how not to" category. But of the ancients, it was the Romans who put the most thought into how to get the most (but not too much) out of one's subordinates, whether it be in a battlefield—or in a wheatfield.

The elder Cato (234–149 B.C.) in a treatise on agriculture—one of the earliest extended bits of Latin prose that we have—provides a checklist of the qualities of the good "agent." The overseer of an estate should be efficient, deferential, loyal, capable of sticking to his authorized budget, and not a devotee of the "Psychic Friends Network."

> He must show good discipline. . . . He must not think that he knows more than the master. His master's friends he must consider as his own. When ordered to listen to someone, he must listen. . . . He must not extend credit to anyone without the master's orders, and he must collect the loans the master has made. As for sowing-seed, fodder, spelt, wine, or oil, he must lend those to no one. He should have a maximum of two or

three households from which he borrows and to which he lends.
. . . He should not wish to buy anything without the master's
knowledge, nor to hide anything from the master. He must
have no hanger-on. He must not consult a fortune-teller, or
diviner, or soothsayer, or astrologer.

—CATO, *ON AGRICULTURE* 5.1–4

Imagine: If Barings Bank had taken a page from Cato, and
limited self-confessed "rogue trader" Nick Leeson to financial
dealings with two or three households, that once-venerable
institution might still be with us today.

When the Skill Mix Is Wrong

When delegation is smooth and effective, we naturally don't
hear much about it. The job gets done, the subordinate ceases
to have authority, and that is that. But dodgy subordinates
occasionally drift from their scripts. In Aesop's collection of
fables is the story of a wolf who daily followed a flock of sheep
and did them no harm, deluding a shepherd into thinking the
wolf was the flock's guardian.

When some business compelled the Shepherd's presence in the
city, he went off leaving the sheep in his charge. The Wolf, seiz-
ing the opportunity, killed the greater part of the flock. When
the Shepherd returned and saw that his flock had been
destroyed, he said: "Well, these are my just desserts. Why did I
entrust sheep to a wolf?"

—AESOP, *FABLES* 165

There's a similar example from the last stage of Rome's
war against Hannibal, in 204 B.C. In that year a certain lowlife
Roman junior officer ordered to garrison a south Italian
town practically brought his superior, the great Scipio
Africanus, to his knees.

Nothing that can make the power of the strong hateful to the weak and defenceless was left undone by Pleminius [chief of the garrison] and his men in their conduct towards the townsmen. Unspeakable outrages were inflicted on their persons, their wives and their children. Their rapacity did not shrink even from sacrilege.

Namely, the troops looted the town's temples, great and small. The situation even degenerated into bloody fighting of Roman against Roman, in which Pleminius and his faction got the worst of it. Scipio made a quick visit to the town to investigate the disturbances, slapped some wrists, but (inexplicably) left Pleminius in charge. Pleminius should have quit while he was ahead. Rather, as soon as his boss left the scene, he conducted his own "trial" of his Roman enemies.

After Pleminius wracked them by every torture which any human body can endure, he had them killed. Yet unsatisfied with the punishment inflicted while they were alive, he had the bodies cast forth unburied. Pleminius exercised a similar cruelty also upon the leading citizens of the town of Locri, who (he had learned) had gone to Publius Scipio to complain of his outrages. . . . But the acts Pleminius perpetrated out of lust and greed . . . created bad reputation and odium not just for him but for his commander-in-chief as well.

—LIVY, *HISTORY OF ROME* 29.9.10–12

For it was a principle among the Romans that a commander might delegate his authority, but not his responsibility, to a nonmagistrate. By not firing this individual when he had the chance, Scipio had to take the damage Pleminius caused on the chin: Livy tells us this great general was almost stripped of his command against the Carthaginians. Instead, Scipio went on to defeat Rome's enemy on their own territory (in 202 B.C.), so ending the Second Punic War—a victory that prompted the senate to vote him the name "Africanus."

Don't Overempower

Fast-forward a little more than 200 years, to the appointment of Sejanus (he of *I, Claudius* fame) as Prefect of the Praetorian Guard in A.D. 14. Stretching his job description to the max, Sejanus tried gradually to worm his way into full partnership (so it seems) with the emperor Tiberius. The emperor meanwhile (to mix metaphors freely) was asleep at the wheel. CEOs or CFOs should beware if the vice president of administration in their organization tallies close to this description:

> Sejanus had a body that could withstand hardships, and a daring spirit. He hid his own designs, while attacking others. He mixed flattery with arrogance. In public, he gave the impression of humility, but deep within he lusted for supremacy. For its sake he was sometimes free-handed and free-wheeling, but more often energetic and watchful—qualities no less dangerous if they are affected with an eye toward sovereignty. He strengthened the previously moderate power of his office by concentrating the cohorts scattered throughout Rome into one camp. . . . Gradually he crept into the soldiers' affections by approaching them and calling them by name. Meanwhile the centurions and tribunes he personally selected.
>
> —TACITUS, *ANNALS* 4.1–2

Eventually, Tiberius was calling Sejanus "partner of my toils"; a sexual intrigue with the emperor's daughter-in-law followed. But once detected in A.D. 31, the liaison proved Sejanus's undoing. The emperor suspected a palace coup, rapidly stripped the praetorian prefect of his position, and saw to his execution.

Who's the Boss?

Sejanus had a perfectly reputable family background, and with all that encouragement from Tiberius, one can understand

how he came to put on airs. It comes as little
surprise, however, that for sensitive tasks subsequent emperors turned increasingly to their
freedmen. These were ex-slaves who had no standing independent of what the imperial house had
given them, so total loyalty could be presumed.
Yet imperial freedmen too could be overem-
powered: The reign of Claudius (A.D. 41–54)
was notorious for it. For instance, while this
emperor was away from Rome, his wife
Messalina "married" her lover Silius in a
macabre ceremony. In the crisis that followed,
we are told it was Narcissus the freedman who
took charge. He filtered all communication to
and from the emperor, and freely gave orders in
Claudius's name. It was Narcissus who conducted the cuckolded Claudius to the lover Silius's
house and who ghost-wrote a speech for
Claudius that whipped up the Praetorian Guard
to demand the punishment of the culprits. The freedman even
quashed Messalina's attempts to win a pardon:

> Claudius had returned home to an early banquet. Then, in a
> softened mood, once he was flush with wine, he gave the order
> to go and tell the "poor woman" (for that's the expression he is
> said to have used) to appear the next day to plead her cause.
> Hearing this . . . Narcissus rushed out, and directed the centuri-
> ons and a military tribune who was present to execute the
> empress, saying that the emperor had ordered it.
>
> —TACITUS, ANNALS 11.37

For this Narcissus received the right to wear a junior senator's insignia. As for Messalina, the senate decreed that not just
her statues but even her name should be removed from all
places, public or private. Yet Narcissus—like all the other

henchmen above—came to a bad end; he was put to death in A.D. 54, on the accession of Claudius's successor Nero.

In truth, freedmen subordinates posed an old and irritating problem for the Roman executive. Cicero does not mince words in telling his brother (a governor of Asia Minor in 61–59 B.C.) precisely why:

> This used to upset me the most: when I kept hearing that your freedman Statius had greater weight with you than your dignified time of life, your governor's rank, and your wisdom demanded. How many people, do you think, have asked me to give them a letter of introduction to Statius? And in talking with me, how many phrases such as "I never approved of that," "I admonished him," "I persuaded him," or "I warned him off" do you think he himself has unselfconciously dropped into conversation? In this situation, even if his reliability is beyond reproach . . . nevertheless the very perception of a freedman or slave enjoying such influence cannot be but at odds with your dignity. Take it from me. . . . Statius has offered all the material for the gossip of those who wish to disparage you.
>
> —CICERO, *LETTERS TO HIS BROTHER QUINTUS* 1.2.3

Delegating the Nasty Stuff

But when push came to shove, freedmen really could come into their own. Cicero's brother had a nasty temper and a habit of relying on unsupervised ghostwriters. So when it was time to leave his province, he badly needed someone to cart some damning memos to the paper shredder:

> Statius told me that they were usually brought to you ready written; he had looked them over, and informed you if they were inequitable. But before he had joined your staff, there had been no culling of correspondence. The result was that there were volumes of select letters which usually met censure. . . . See to it,

finding men devoted to you (an easy task), that the following classes of letters are destroyed: first, inequitable ones; second, those that are contradictory; third, those written in a foolish or unusual manner; and fourth, those that are abusive against anyone.

—CICERO, *LETTERS TO HIS BROTHER QUINTUS* 1.2.8–9

According to Xenophon, the early-fifth-century poet Simonides advised a leader simply to let the buck stop with his hatchet men. In other words, delegate to others the task of punishing those who need it, but keep for yourself the privilege of giving out prizes:

When it comes to a ruler's activities, it seems to me that some lead very much to the deepest unpopularity, while others win great gratitude. Teaching the people what things are best, and praising and honoring individuals who nobly accomplish these very things, this activity generates gratitude. However, rebuking individuals who come up short in their actions, and exercising coercion, inflicting fines and punishing them, these activities necessarily incur people's enmity.

—XENOPHON, *HIERO* 9.1–2

Aristotle offers a more nuanced view of how delegates should do the dirty work:

The less odium involved for those who inflict punishment, the more effectively judgments will run their course. So there is twofold odium if the same magistrates who imposed the sentence also execute it. And if the same ones execute it in all cases, they are the enemies of everyone.

—ARISTOTLE, *POLITICS* 1322A

Failure to observe these principles in 63 B.C. put the Roman statesman Cicero in hot water. As one of the two consuls (that is, chief magistrates) of that year, he had faced down an alleged conspiracy—the seriousness of which was debated even in antiquity—led by one Catiline. Put simply, Catiline was a frustrated politician of distinguished lineage who in his own repeated bids to reach high office had accumulated a mountain of debt. In time he assembled a coterie of similarly disgruntled, insolvent folks—both men and women—all with a view to shaking up the status quo through means fair or foul. Cicero succeeded in convincing the senate that Catiline and his crew had to be stopped, whatever the cost. That involved putting actual armies into the field, which is how (eventually) Catiline met his end. Few tears will have been shed over that rascal's death in January 62. But people simply did not think it good form for Cicero late in his consulship to preside over a debate in the Roman Senate on the punishment of a bunch of Catiline's followers (some of whom were quite well connected), and then personally to see to their prompt execution. Four years later the incident could be used as a pretext to drive Cicero into exile. Though Cicero managed to secure a return to Rome after a little more than a year, he remained defensive until the end of his life (43 B.C.) about this bold decision to inflict capital punishment en masse outside the court system.

Don't Underempower

Remember the "Sorcerer's Apprentice" from Walt Disney's *Fantasia*? The prototype, courtesy of the self-described "Syrian Greek" Lucian (writing circa A.D. 150), shows vividly the bad things that can happen when a subordinate lacks the wherewithal for a task. Here a traveler tells how, on a trip up the Nile, he befriended the holy man Pancrates, who shared all of his secret knowledge with him—well, almost all.

Whenever we came to a stopping-place, the man used to take either the bar of the door or the broom or even the pestle, throw clothes on it, recite a certain spell over it, and make it walk, seeming to everyone else to be a man. Going off, it would draw water and buy food and prepare it and in every way skillfully serve and wait upon us. Then, when he had his fill of its services, he would again make the broom a broom or the pestle a pestle, reciting another spell over it. Though I was most eager, I was not able to learn this from him. For he was jealous, although most accomodating in other respects. But one day I overheard the spell, escaping notice by standing in the dark. . . . On the next day, when he was seeing to some business in the marketplace, I took the pestle, dressed it up in the same way, said the spell over it, and ordered it to carry water.

—LUCIAN, *LOVER OF LIES* 35–36

The result: disaster. When the traveler couldn't keep the wooden pestle from flooding the house, he took an ax and cut it in two—only to see each part take up a jar and continue the work. Fortunately, Pancrates soon showed up and (literally) bailed out his apprentice.

But Never, Never Give It All Up

Should the wizard have shared all his proprietary information? From his perspective, he had nothing to gain from it. Similarly, the executive never gives up all his or her authority in delegating power. For this ancient principle, the most vivid illustration is a story from Rome's fighting against Gauls and the Samnites of central Italy (295 B.C.). When things looked as if they were going against Rome in a particularly savage battle, Publius Decius, one of the two consuls (heads of state), carried on a family tradition of ritualistic self-sacrifice—what the Romans called "devotion," a way of calling the wrath of the gods onto the military standards, armor, and weapons of the enemy. Yet before immolating himself, this general first ordered the priest who had helped him recite the solemn and terrible prayer of "devotion" to take his insignia and to step into his command. But not as consul: The priest was delegated only second-level powers, at the rank of what the Romans called a "praetor." (The praetor was a high-ranking magistrate, but one in permanent subordination to the consuls.) It is hard to see why Decius, before he spurred on his horse to charge right into the center of the Gauls' line of battle, did not let the priest have 100 percent of his authority—especially since he meant him to take over his own army. He must have been legally prevented from doing so. Many examples from subsequent history confirm that was the case.

Transitioning from VP to CEO

The story of the assassination of Rome's fifth king, Tarquin (sixth century B.C.), must have seemed more than a bit silly to ancients who knew their Roman constitutional law—in particular, the prohibition on full delegation of one's power, discussed above. The tale goes like this. To stave off a hostile takeover by the assassins (sons of king number four, Ancus Marcius), Tarquin's queen Tanaquil makes out to the Roman people that her husband had survived but delegated all his power to her son-in-law, Servius Tullius:

> Servius appeared in public wearing the regal robe of state and accompanied by his official attendants. Seating himself in the royal chair, he decided some cases and pretended about others that he would consult the king. So for several days after Tarquin had given up the ghost, Servius covered up the death and strengthened his own position through his fiction of exercising delegated authority. Finally, the reality of the situation became clear when sounds of mourning arose in the palace. Protected by a strong bodyguard, Servius was the first who ruled Rome without being elected by the People, though he did have the approval of the Senate.

—LIVY, *HISTORY OF ROME* 1.41.6

That turned out to be a seamless succession by a favored subordinate; were it not for Tanaquil's quick thinking and Servius's passable acting, Rome might have been plunged into serious internecine strife, thanks to the existence of the rival faction that assassinated Tarquin. Yet examples of rougher transitions abound. For instance, around the year 522 B.C., the eastern Mediterranean Greek island of Samos found itself ruled by a certain Maeandrius. The magnificent tyrant Polycrates had delegated this man authority before leaving for a trip to the mainland—a trip from which he never returned. When the surrogate learned that the Persians had crucified Polycrates for his independent ambitions, he first set up an altar with precinct to the god Zeus the Liberator. An assembly of the citizens was then called. Here's a speech that the historian Herodotus puts in his mouth:

> To me, as you know, have been entrusted Polycrates' scepter and all of his power, and it is in my power now to rule you. But what I criticize in my neighbor, I shall not do myself, so far as I am able. I did not approve when Polycrates played the despot over men like himself, nor when any other man does such things. Polycrates has met his personal destiny; I proclaim equality, making his power public. The only rewards I claim for myself, are that six talents [that is, for all practical purposes, $6 million] of Polycrates' wealth be set apart for me, and in addition for myself and my descendants I lay claim to the priesthood of Zeus the Liberator, for whom I have built a temple. And freedom I confer upon you.
>
> —HERODOTUS, *HISTORIES* 3.142

According to Herodotus, someone then rose up in the crowd and answered: "Well, you are not even worthy to rule us, you low-born living plague. But you had better give an account of the cash that you have handled."

It's tough for a subordinate to step overnight into his or her boss's shoes. Maeandrius for his part quickly dropped his "nice guy" approach and chose the iron fist instead. But he didn't last long, soon having to cede the prosperous island to the covetous Persians.

The Decentralized Office

Let's move from Samos to a macropicture. All the great ancient imperial powers—the Persians, Athenians, Macedonians, and the Romans—had organization charts. Each level of management's support structure had its own role to play. But how does one communicate orders when delegatees are dispersed far and wide, and the days of intranets, skypaging, and videoconferences are still some millennia to come? As we have seen, the Romans had a particularly sophisticated communications network. The emperor himself had ultimate oversight of the postmasters in the various provinces. Communications were felt to be so good that governors might refer even minor problems back to command central:

> If they feel even a little doubt about their subjects' lawsuits and petitions, public or private, they immediately send to the Emperor and ask what ought to be done. And they wait until he gives a sign, just like a chorus waits for its director. So he need not wear himself out traversing the entire Empire, or visiting a series of peoples to shore up each individual place whenever he sets foot in their country. Rather, it is quite easy for the Emperor to sit and manage the whole world by correspondence; his letters are practically no sooner written than delivered, as if by airmail.
>
> —AELIUS ARISTIDES, *ORATION TO ROME* 60

There is a whole book of such letters between the emperor Trajan and Pliny the Younger, his governor of Bithynia and Pontus (modern north Turkey). It includes correspondence between Pliny and Trajan (circa A.D. 110) on how to cope with the rise of a new religion in his province—Christianity.

It is a fixed rule for me, Lord, to refer to you all things about which I am uncertain. For who is better able either to set right my doubts or to inform my ignorance? I never have been present at judicial inquiries regarding Christians, and for that reason I do not know what is the customary method and extent of either punishing or investigating them. . . . It seemed to me a matter worthy of consultation, especially given the number of those at risk. For many of every age, of every social station, and also of both sexes are being summoned or will be summoned to trial.

—PLINY THE YOUNGER, *LETTERS* 10.106.1, 9

In this letter, the governor provides a self-aggrandizing description of his investigations and legal procedures concerning this sect. The emperor's reply to Pliny confirms his basic decisions not to hunt down the Christians, but of those brought before him, to pardon those who recant their beliefs.

14

Handling Success and Coping with Mistakes

It is well to remember that all achievement is fraught with danger. The CEO who does everything right, who reaches the very pinnacle of success, must nevertheless remain on guard. For human frailty is such, we're told, that success can pave the way for downfall, and once disaster has been set in motion, haste and passion and senseless folly can hasten one's plummet.

Don't Let Success Go to Your Head

Now, Julius Caesar was a very smart fellow. He discerned how to exploit weaknesses in the declining republic of Rome and accrue power for himself. He enjoyed greatness. In fact, he enjoyed it too much: He found the adoration of the populace profoundly gratifying. The more acclaim Caesar received, the harder it was to seem humble. At the same time, certain high-ranking Romans who resented Caesar's success could not fail to note his growing arrogance. Although Caesar was not a king, he was starting to behave like one. The following passage from Suetonius recounts one of the key events leading up to Caesar's assassination in 44 B.C.:

> At the Latin Festival, as he was returning amid the unrestrained and novel acclamation of the people, someone in the crowd placed on his statue a laurel wreath with a white fillet tied to it [which signified royalty]; and when the tribunes of the plebs, Epidius Marullus and Caesetius Flavus, ordered that the ribbon be taken off the crown and that the man be led away in chains, Caesar heavily upbraided them and deprived them of their power. . . . Nor from that time on could he dispel the infamy of having aspired to the title of king.
>
> —SUETONIUS, *LIFE OF JULIUS CAESAR* 79.1–2

The fate of Julius Caesar reveals the folly of arrogance. The fate of Philip II of Macedon, on the other hand, shows that success should not make one careless. Philip, the father of Alexander the Great, was the man whose discipline and raw determination united the splintered kingdom of Macedon in the mid-fourth-century B.C. and transformed it into the fore-most military power in the region. He armed his foot soldiers with sixteen-foot-long pikes; fighting in formation, they were untouchable, invincible. Philip fought alongside them, distinguishing himself in battle over and over. He suffered many wounds, including a crippling blow to the thigh and the loss of an eye. Indeed, he achieved so much and defied death so often that he must have thought nothing could kill him. Big mistake. In 336 B.C., at his daughter's wedding, he confidently dismissed his bodyguards—the Macedonian equivalent to the Secret Service—and this proved fatal:

> When the theater was full, Philip himself entered wearing a white cloak. As instructed, his spear bearers followed at a distance, for Philip was trying to prove to everyone that he was

guarded by the common goodwill of the Greeks and had no need of a guard of spear bearers. So great a distinction he enjoyed; but as all congratulated him and called him happy, unexpectedly and without warning the plot against the king was revealed—and with it, death. . . . Having stationed his horses at the gates, [Pausanias, the assassin] came to the entrance of the theater carrying a concealed Celtic dagger. When Philip ordered the friends who were with him to go ahead into the theater, and while the spear bearers kept their distance, [Pausanias] saw that the king was alone, rushed at him, sent the blade home through his ribs, and stretched him out dead.

—DIODORUS THE SICILIAN,
LIBRARY OF UNIVERSAL HISTORY 16.93.1–2, 94.3

The meteoric career of Alexander the Great, finally, suggests that success can change one's nature for the worse. Having embarked on his path of world conquest in 334 B.C., when he was barely out of his teens, Alexander rose all too quickly to dizzying heights of military and political power. Only four years later he was hailed as conquerer of the vast and enormously wealthy Persian empire and came to regard himself as semi-divine. He claimed descent from Heracles and even Zeus, the top deity in the Greek pantheon, and later he allegedly expected people in the Greek cities back home to worship him. Meanwhile, out there in Asia, Alexander was starting to make mistakes:

Alexander had begun to act precipitously in inflicting punishments and also in believing unfavorable reports; plainly, success can change one's nature, and rarely is anyone cautious enough with respect to his own good fortune.

—QUINTUS CURTIUS RUFUS,
HISTORY OF ALEXANDER 10.1.39–40

Alexander should have known better. He had, after all, been tutored by the philosopher Aristotle, who preached moderation in all things.

Don't Boast

Pliny the Younger observes that self-praise is bound to arouse resentment, and advises against mentioning one's own good deeds and achievements:

> Truly, even praise offered by others seldom finds a favorable reception—and how hard to frame a speech about oneself or own's own family that does not offend the critics! The only accomplishments that we don't twist or slander are those that are laid to rest in obscurity and silence. . . . So the deed that is splendid if reported by a third party turns into nothing if recounted by the person who did it.

—PLINY THE YOUNGER, *LETTERS* 1.8.6, 15

What Pliny forgets to explain, unfortunately, is how to climb the corporate ladder without bragging—a rare if not impossible feat. He also fails to consider certain occasions when a person might need to blow his own horn very loudly to save his skin. Fortunately, the great Greek moralist Plutarch (roughly A.D. 50–120) fills the gap:

> First, self-praise is blameless if you do it in defending yourself against slander or accusation. . . . For at such a time, one not only escapes pretension and emptiness and ostentation in saying something solemn about oneself, but one also shows strength of will and greatness of character.

—PLUTARCH, MORALIA,
ON INOFFENSIVE SELF-PRAISE 540C

Be Realistic Enough to Accept Mistakes . . .

If success can lead to arrogance, it can also lead to unrealistic expectations and intolerance for other people's faults and failings. It is Xenophon's idealized Cyrus the Great who reminds us that everybody makes mistakes:

> Brave men and allies, what happened is human—for that men should make mistakes, I think, is in no way strange.
>
> —XENOPHON, *EDUCATION OF CYRUS* 5.4.19

And Pliny the Younger, arguing that one must forgive, quotes the philosopher Thrasea Paetus, an opponent of arbitrary government:

> Let us keep in mind what Thrasea, the mildest of men and for that reason also the greatest, often used to say: "Who hates faults, hates mankind."
>
> —PLINY THE YOUNGER, *LETTERS* 8.22.2–3

. . . but Try Not to Make Them

It's clear, however, that mistakes can be dangerous, as the statesman Pericles warned his fellow Athenians at the outset of war against Sparta:

> I dread our own mistakes more than the enemy's intentions.
>
> —THUCYDIDES, *THE PELOPONNESIAN WAR* 1.144.1

Learn from Your Past Blunders

If you've made mistakes, then try to learn from them in time to prevent the next round of disaster. In 431 B.C., Sparta and

Athens fell into a protracted conflict known to us as the Peloponnesian War. Sparta was at that time a supremely disciplined land power that dominated mainland Greece; Athens had become a great sea power with an impressive armada and many possessions and allies abroad. Not long into the war, and after a calamitous defeat in the Gulf of Corinth, the Spartans realized that they and their Peloponnesian allies would have to improve their naval tactics. In the following passage from Thucydides, the charismatic Brasidas and another Spartan general rally their forces before the next sea battle with this advice:

> Against their greater experience marshall your greater daring.
> . . . We cannot find a single reason why we should fail; and as many mistakes as we made before, now these same events will teach us a lesson.
>
> THUCYCIDES, *THE PELOPONNESIAN WAR* 2.87.7

Use Spin Control

But no one is perfect. Luckily, it's almost as good to hide your mistakes as not to make them, as one episode in the career of Alexander the Great will show. He lost one battle in a costly and potentially embarrassing way, but quickly covered up:

> In that battle 2,000 infantry and 300 horsemen fell. This disaster Alexander concealed with a shrewd stratagem, threatening with death those who had returned from the battle, if they divulged what had happened.
>
> —QUINTUS CURTIUS RUFUS,
> *HISTORY OF ALEXANDER* 7.7.39

Most of the Roman consuls and emperors could have benefited greatly from a modern team of spin control experts. They constantly faced one crisis or another—whether the slave rebellion led by Spartacus or civil strife or the eruption of Mount Vesuvius that buried Pompeii or flood or famine or yet another border incident with those damned barbarians. Emperors always tried, of course, to put the best face on their efforts, awarding themselves triumphal processions to celebrate military victories, for example, or putting their profiles on coins whose flip side said, "Peace." After coping with any great natural or man-made disaster, a clever leader would try to remind the populace that he had been the one to arrange additional shipments of foreign grain and so forth. One of the most notorious incidents in Nero's reign as emperor of Rome was the great fire of A.D. 64, which devastated much of the capital city. As the historian Tacitus tells it, Nero actually initiated relief efforts for the thousands of people left homeless by the fire—but then bungled his public relations effort:

> Nor was it possible to stop [the fire] before it devoured the Palatine and the Esquiline house and everything around them. But as a relief to the homeless and fugitive populace, [Nero] opened the Field of Mars [level land next to the Tiber], the buildings of Agrippa [which included a granary], and even his own Gardens, and built hasty shelters, which received the destitute masses. The necessities of life were brought up from Ostia and nearby municipalities, and the price of grain was lowered to three sesterces. Yet these popular measures turned out to be wasted, for the rumor had spread that while the city was burning, [Nero] had entered onto his private stage and had sung about the ruin of Troy.
>
> —TACITUS, *ANNALS* 15.39

Nowadays Nero is said to have fiddled as Rome burned. Actually, there weren't any fiddles back then, but Nero liked to sing, and playing the cithara, an ancient stringed instrument, was central to his identity, so there's something to the story after all.

Learn to Cope with Disappointment

A frequent theme in Greek literature concerns the dramatic and irreversible fall from fortune of the wildly successful man who thought he had it all. Bill Gates, are you listening? But even if a high-ranking executive faces no major blows, there are bound to be some minor disappointments along the way. If so, one needs to deal with them in a mature, constructive fashion, without childish temper tantrums or irrational behavior. With a little temperance and forethought, anyone can surely do better than the Persian king Xerxes, who came up with a completely dysfunctional response when a storm wrecked his first bridge across the Hellespont, the ribbon of water that separates Asia from Europe:

> As soon as the strait had been bridged, a great storm fell upon it and cut the cables and broke them up. When Xerxes learned this, he became furious and ordered that the Hellespont be lashed with three hundred strokes and that a pair of fetters be lowered into it. Indeed, . . . he also sent branders to brand the Hellespont. And he instructed those who did the lashing to say barbarous and presumptuous things: "Oh, bitter water, our master lays this punishment on you because you wronged him though he never did you wrong. And King Xerxes will cross you, whether you like it or not."
>
> —HERODOTUS, *HISTORIES* 7.34–35

According to Herodotus, such disgraceful behavior was typical of Xerxes. It was precisely this sort of arrogant posturing, in fact, that energized the king's Greek adversaries and led to his ignominious defeat. So the moral, perhaps, is that the CEO should stay in touch with all the practical wisdom that enabled him or her to succeed in the first place.

SIGNIFICANT
ANCIENT AUTHORS AND
HISTORICAL FIGURES

Aelius Aristides. Orator and writer from Asia Minor, second century A.D.

Aeschylus. Greek tragic playwright, early fifth century B.C.

Aesop. Legendary author of Greek fables with speaking animals, sixth century B.C.?

Alcibiades. Athenian politician and general, lived circa 450–403 B.C.

Alexander the Great. Macedonian conqueror, lived 356–323 B.C.

Alexander Severus. Roman emperor, ruled A.D. 222–235

Anacreon. Greek lyric poet from island of Teos, late sixth century B.C.

Antiochus III "the Great." Seleucid king, lived circa 242–187 B.C.

Antiochus IV. Son and successor of Antiochus the Great, lived circa 215–164 B.C.

Antiphanes. Greek comic playwright of Middle Comedy, fourth century B.C.

Antiphon. Athenian orator, later fifth century B.C.

Antoninus Pius. Roman emperor, ruled A.D. 138–61

Appian. Greek historian from Alexandria, early second century A.D.

Archilochus. Greek mercenary and poet from island of Paros, seventh century B.C.

Aristophanes. Greek playwright and master of Old Comedy, late fifth and early fourth century B.C.

Aristotle. Greek philosopher, lived 384–322 B.C.

Arrian. Greek historian from Nicomedia in Bithynia, late first to mid–second century A.D.

Augustus. First Roman emperor, ruled as such 27 B.C. to A.D. 14

Bacchylides. Greek lyric poet from island of Ceos, early fifth century B.C.

Caligula. Emperor of Rome, ruled A.D. 37–41

Cambyses. Persian king, ruled 530–522 B.C.

Caracalla. Roman emperor, ruled A.D. 198–217

Cassius Dio. Greek historian and public figure in Rome, late second and early third century A.D.

Catiline. Roman noble who led armed conspiracy against government in 63 B.C.

Cato the Elder, or "the Censor." Roman statesman, lived 234–149 B.C.

Cicero. First century B.C. Roman statesman and orator, lived 106–43 B.C.

Claudian. Roman poet from Alexandria, writing circa A.D. 400

Claudius. Roman emperor, ruled A.D. 41–54

Cleopatra VII. Queen of Egypt, last of the Ptolemies, lived 69–30 B.C.

Commodus. Roman emperor, ruled A.D. 180–192

Crassus. Roman plutocrat (active 87–53) who famously allied with Pompey and Caesar in the 50s B.C.

Croesus. Fabulously wealthy last king of Lydia, defeated by Persians in 546 B.C.

Curtius Rufus. Roman rhetorician and historian of Alexander the Great, wrote first century A.D.

Cyrus the Great. Persian king whose conquests created a vast empire, died 530 B.C.

Darius I. Persian king, ruled 522–486 B.C., who unsuccessfully invaded Greece, 490 B.C.

Darius III. Persian king conquered by Alexander the Great, died 330 B.C.

Demosthenes. Greek statesman and orator, lived 384–322 B.C.

Diocletian. Roman emperor, ruled A.D. 284–305

Diodorus Siculus. Greek historian from Sicily, first century B.C.

Domitian. Roman emperor, ruled A.D. 81–96

Epictetus. Stoic philosopher, late first–early second century A.D.

Frontinus. Roman technocrat, wrote late first and early second century A.D.

Fronto. Roman orator and senator, second century A.D.

Galba. Roman emperor, ruled A.D. 68–69

Gelon. Ruler of Syracuse in Sicily, early fifth century B.C.

Germanicus. Heir apparent of the emperor Tiberius, lived circa 15 B.C.–A.D. 19

Hadrian. Roman emperor, ruled A.D. 117–138

Hannibal. Carthaginian general (247–182) who invaded Italy in 218 B.C., launching the Second Punic War.

Herodotus. Greek historian from Halicarnassus in southwestern Asia Minor, mid-fifth century B.C.

Hesiod. Greek didactic poet, circa 700 B.C.

Hippocrates. Greek physician, fifth century B.C.

Homer. Legendary eighth-century Greek poet to whom the *Iliad* and *Odyssey* are attributed.

Horace. Roman poet during age of Augustus, first century B.C.

Isocrates. Athenian orator, lived 436–338 B.C.

Josephus. Jewish historian, born 37/8 A.D.

Julius Caesar. Roman general and dictator, lived 100–44 B.C.

Livy. Roman historian, late first century B.C. and early first A.D.

Lucian. Writer and philosopher active at Athens, second century A.D.

Lysias. Athenian orator, lived 459–380 B.C.

Marc Antony. Roman politician and general, joined with Cleopatra to fight against Octavian, died 30 B.C.

Marcus Aurelius. Roman emperor and Stoic philosopher, ruled A.D. 161–180

Marius. Roman general and politician, lived circa 157–86 B.C.

Menander. Greek comic playwright of New Comedy, late fourth to early third centuries B.C.

Messalina. Wife of the Roman emperor Claudius, died A.D. 48

Mithridates VI, king of Pontus and formidable Roman enemy, ruled 120–63 B.C.

Nepos. Roman biographer, later first century B.C.

Nero. Roman emperor, ruled A.D. 54–68

Nicias. Athenian statesman and general (470–413 B.C.) during Peloponnesian War

Octavian. Rome's first emperor, who renamed himself Augustus (see above).

Onasander. Author of Greek treatise on generalship, first century A.D.

Pericles. Statesman and general who led the Athenians starting circa 462 B.C. until his death in 429 B.C.

Phaedrus. Author of Latin verse fables, first century A.D.

Philip II. King of Macedon and father of Alexander the Great, ruled 360–336 B.C.

Pindar. Greek lyric poet, early fifth century B.C.

Plato. Greek philosopher, lived circa 429–347 B.C.

Plautus. Roman comic playwright, late third and early second century B.C.

Pliny the Younger. Roman magistrate and writer, A.D. 61–112

Plutarch. Greek biographer and moralist, died circa A.D. 120

Polyaenus. Macedonian rhetorician, author of book of Stratagems, mid–second century A.D.

Polybius. Greek historian of Rome's rise to world dominion, lived second century B.C.

Polycrates. Tyrant of Greek island of Samos, sixth century B.C.

Pyrrhus. King of Epirus; scored costly victories against Romans, early third century B.C.

Pythagoras. Greek philosopher and mathematician, late sixth century B.C.

Sallust. Roman historian, first century B.C.

Scipio Aemilianus. Roman general (185–129) who sacked Carthage, 146 B.C.

Scipio Africanus. Roman general and statesman (236–183) who defeated Hannibal in 202 B.C.

Seneca. Stoic philosopher writing in the time of Nero, died A.D. 65

Sertorius, rebel Roman governor of Spain, died 72 B.C.

Socrates. Athenian philosopher, lived 469–399 B.C.

Solon. Athenian lawmaker circa 594/3 B.C.

Spartacus. Ex-gladiator who led slave rebellion in Italy 73–71 B.C.

Statius. Roman poet, first century A.D.

Suetonius. Roman biographer, late first and early second century A.D.

Tacitus. Roman historian, late first to early second centuries A.D.

Tarquin the Proud. Last king of Rome, ruled 534–510 B.C.

Theognis. Greek elegiac poet, sixth century B.C.

Themistocles. Statesman (528–462) who spearheaded development of Athenian navy, early fifth century B.C.

Thucydides. Greek historian of the Peloponnesian War, lived circa 460–399 B.C.

Titus. Roman emperor, ruled A.D. 79–81

Trajan. Roman emperor, ruled A.D. 98–117

Vespasian. Roman emperor, ruled A.D. 69–79

Xerxes I. Persian king, ruled 486–465 B.C., who unsuccessfully invaded Greece, 480–479 B.C.

Xenophon. Greek historian, lived circa 428–354 B.C.

IMPORTANT DATES

BEFORE COMMON ERA OR B.C.

2800–1000	Bronze Age in Aegean Sea region
1600–1100	Late Bronze (Helladic) Age/Mycenaean Period: setting for Heroic myths
1100–900	Early Greek Dark Age: emergence of Homeric (aristocratic) society
900–750	Late Dark Age: poems of Homer *(Iliad, Odyssey)* and Hesiod *(Works and Days)* take shape
776	Traditional date for founding of the Olympic Games
775–550	Great age of Greek colonization
753	Traditional date for the foundation of Rome (Roman kings)
from 750	Beginning of Greek Archaic period; return of literacy; city-state governments begin

circa 650	Archilochus active as poet
650–625	Spartans fight Second Messenian War, helped by poetry of Tyrtaeus
620–480	Poems attributed to Theognis composed at Megara
616–579	Tarquin the Elder is king of Rome
600–550	First collections of the *Fables* of Aesop
594–593	Solon legislates his reforms at Athens; movement toward democracy begins
578–535	Servius Tullius king of Rome
569–525	Pharaoh Amasis revives Egypt and resists Persians
559–530	Cyrus is first Persian "Great King" and ruler of Middle East
545–500	Anacreon composes his poems about drinking, womanizing, and the "good life"
534–510	Tarquin the Proud is the last Roman king
509	Roman Republic founded
508–507	Cleisthenes restores and extends "popular" government at Athens
499–492	Ionian Revolt: eastern Greeks try to throw off Persian rule
498–438	Pindar composes his poems in honor of aristocratic athletic victors
495–456	Aeschylus composes his tragedies at Athens

493–472	Themistocles builds up Athenian military power and democracy
490	Athenians defeat Persians at Marathon
486–465	Xerxes, Great King of the Persians, reigns
485–431	Bacchylides, master of lyric poetry, is active
480	Great Persian invasion of Greece under King Xerxes; Persians defeated in battle at Salamis by Themistocles; beginning of Classical Period in Greece
479	Persians driven back from European Greece
478	Foundation of Delian League against the Persians by the Athenians
468–406	Sophocles produces his tragedies at Athens
462–461	Democracy becomes predominant at Athens
462–429	Pericles' political career at Athens
454–420	Herodotus at work on his *Histories*
451–450	Law code of Twelve Tables at Rome
447	Parthenon temple to Athena begun at Athens
431–404	Great Peloponnesian War between Athens and Sparta
428–427	Mytilene unsuccessfully revolts from Athens
427–385	Aristophanes, the master of "Old Comedy," produces his plays
425–404	Athenian Alcibiades politically and militarily active

431–399	Thucydides composes his *Histories* on Peloponnesian War
415	Sacrilege against sacred mysteries at Athens
415–413	Disastrous expedition of the Athenians against Sicily
407–375	Lysias composes legal speeches at Athens
403–402	Civil war in Athens between Thirty Tyrants and democratic forces
400–354	Political and literary career of Xenophon: *Socratic Memoirs* (circa 381), *Household Manager* (362–361), *Education of Cyrus* (360s), *Ways and Means* (355–354)
400–347	Philosophical works of Plato
399	Execution of Socrates
394	General warfare resumes in Greece
390s–340s	Speeches (essays) of Isocrates composed at Athens
371	Thebans decisively defeat Spartans at Battle of Leuctra
367	Laws of Licinius and Sextius at Rome; end of sharpest political struggle between classes
359–336	King Philip II builds up Macedonian empire: *Philippic History* of Theopompus
355–322	Political career and speeches (including *Philippics*) of Demosthenes against Macedonians
347–322	Aristotle produces his philosophical works

343–290	Rome fights Samnite Wars for control of Italy
338	Defeat of Athenians and Thebans at Chaeroneia by Philip II; Macedonian dominance over Greece
336–323	Reign of Alexander (III) the Great, Macedonian king and conqueror of Near East
334	Alexander invades Asia
331	Alexander conquers Egypt and founds Alexandria
330	Alexander in control of Iran
327–325	Alexander's campaign in India
323	Hellenistic period begins (death of Alexander)
321–289	Menander, master of Attic New Comedy, produces his plays
280–275	Greek dynast, King Pyrrhus of Epirus, fails to break Roman hold over Italy
264–241	First Punic War between Rome and Carthage
218–201	Second Punic War between Rome and Carthage (Hannibal invades Italy)
210–184	Plautus produces his comic plays at Rome
203–149	Public and literary career of Marcus Porcius Cato the Elder ("Cato the Censor")
202	Publius Cornelius Scipio Africanus defeats Hannibal at Zama

192–188	Roman-Syrian War; Publius and Lucius Scipio victorious over Seleucid ruler over Near East, Antiochus III (189)
184	Accusations against and retirement of Publius Cornelius Scipio Africanus
175–164	Reign of Seleucid king Antiochus IV, invader of Egypt and persecutor of the Jews
150–118	Production of the *Histories* of Polybius
146	Roman general, Scipio Aemilianus, destroys Carthage
146	Romans destroy Greek city of Corinth (Hellenistic Period ends)
133	Tribunate of Tiberius Sempronius Gracchus
107–86	Gaius Marius is intermittently dominant political and military leader at Rome
87–53	Political career of Marcus Licinius Crassus, member of the First Triumvirate
81–43	Political career (with orations) and other treatises of Marcus Tullius Cicero
82–79	Dictatorship and domination of Sulla at Rome
82–72	Sertorius's separatism from Rome in Spain
73–71	Slave rebellion in Italy of Spartacus
73–44	Political career of Julius Caesar
67	Pompey the Great clears the eastern Mediterranean of pirates
66–63	Pompey conquers King Mithridates VI of Pontus

63	Cicero as consul suppresses the Catiline conspiracy
60–30	Didorus Siculus compiles his *Library of Universal History*
59	First consulship of Julius Caesar
58–50	Caesar conquers Gaul (modern France and Belgium)
51–30	Reign of Cleopatra (VII), last Ptolemaic ruler of Greek Egypt
44	Julius Caesar is assassinated on Ides of March
38–13	Horace composes his poetry
31	Octavian (later Augustus) defeats Antony and Cleopatra at Actium
27–A.D. 14	Principate of Augustus, first Roman emperor
27–A.D. 12	Livy writes his history of Rome
18	*Aeneid* published after death of Virgil

COMMON ERA OR A.D.

9	Germans massacre Roman legions in Teutoberg forest
10–50	Phaedrus reworks Greek fables at Rome
14–37	Tiberius is emperor at Rome
14–31	Sejanus (leading agent of Tiberius) commands Praetorian Guard
37–41	Reign of the emperor Caligula

40–65	Literary career of Seneca, teacher and adviser to Nero
41–54	Claudius is Roman emperor
40–54	Quintus Curtius Rufus composes *History of Alexander*; Onasander writes on generalship
54–68	Nero is Roman emperor
64	Great fire and persecution of the Christians at Rome
68–69	Short reign of Galba at Rome
69	Year of the Four Emperors
78–85	Gnaeus Julius Agricola finishes Roman conquests in Britain
85–120	Epictetus active as philosopher
86–98	Martial publishes his epigrams
89–96	Poet Statius active at Rome under the emperor Domitian
90–112	Pliny the Younger active as politician and letter writer (*Panegyric Oration*: 100)
90–120	Plutarch writes his *Moral Essays* and *Parallel Lives* of Greek and Roman statesmen
96–115	Tacitus writes his *Histories* and *Annals*
98–117	Trajan is emperor; greatest extent of Roman empire
110–120	Suetonius publishes his *Lives of the Caesars*
117–138	Hadrian is emperor

110–145	Career of Arrian, Roman statesman and historian of Alexander
138–161	Antoninus Pius emperor
140–166	Marcus Cornelius Fronto is active as writer and statesman
144–180s	Writings of Aelius Aristides
160–180s	Lucian of Samosata writes dialogues and philosophical essays
161–180	Marcus Aurelius is Roman emperor
180–192	Commodus, son of Marcus Aurelius, rules Roman empire
195–240	Public career of statesman and historian Cassius Dio
211–217	Caracalla is emperor
218–222	Reign of Elagabalus
222–235	Alexander Severus is emperor
236–284	Period of great upheaval and disorder (with some respites) in Roman empire
284–305	Emperor Diocletian reorganizes Roman empire
306–337	Constantine emperor: creation of Christian empire
390–404	Poet Claudian works at Rome
476	End of Roman empire in West

INDEX